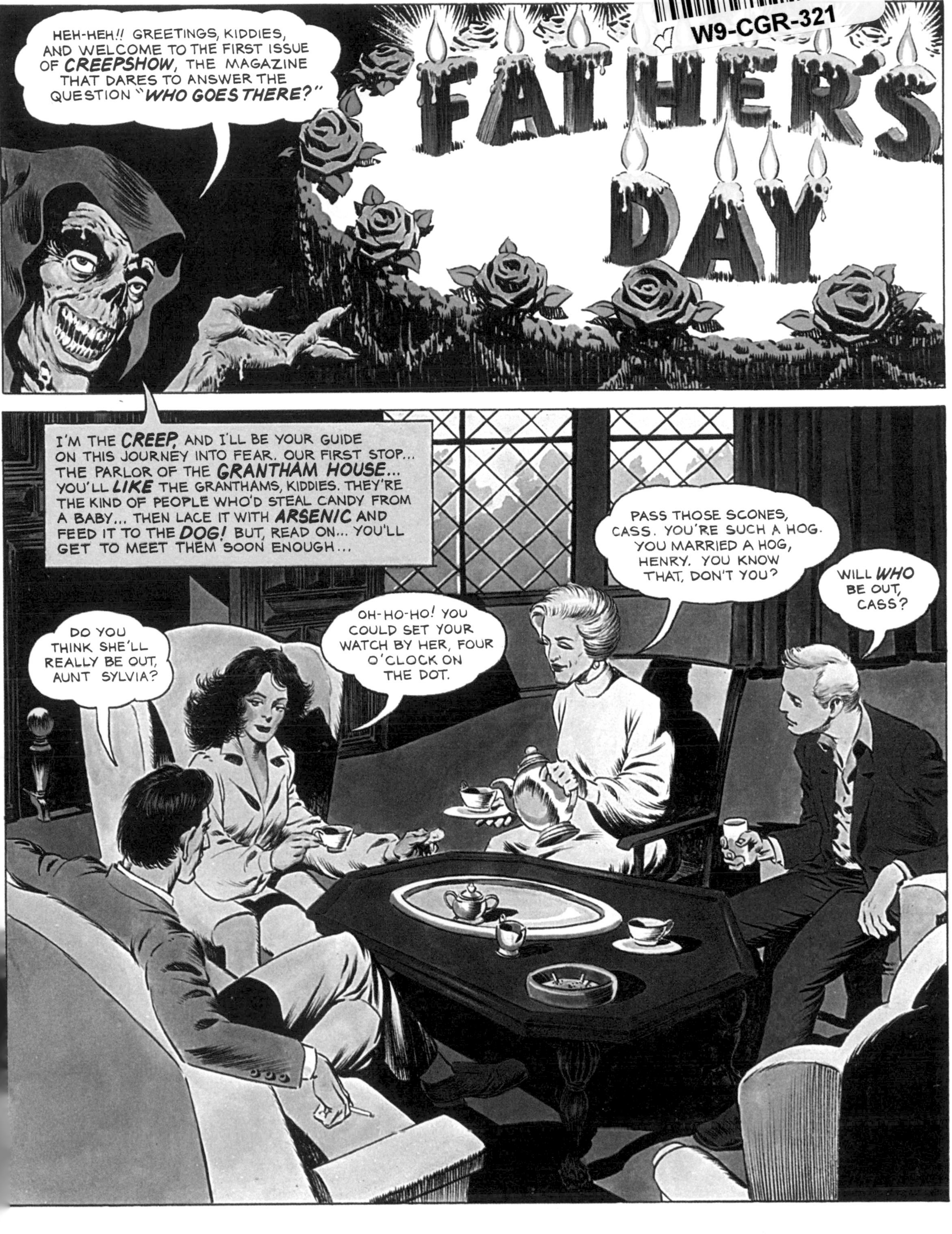
HEH-HEH!! GREETINGS, KIDDIES, AND WELCOME TO THE FIRST ISSUE OF CREEPSHOW, THE MAGAZINE THAT DARES TO ANSWER THE QUESTION "WHO GOES THERE?"
FATHER'S DAY
I'M THE CREEP, AND I'LL BE YOUR GUIDE ON THIS JOURNEY INTO FEAR. OUR FIRST STOP... THE PARLOR OF THE GRANTHAM HOUSE... YOU'LL LIKE THE GRANTHAMS, KIDDIES. THEY'RE THE KIND OF PEOPLE WHO'D STEAL CANDY FROM A BABY... THEN LACE IT WITH ARSENIC AND FEED IT TO THE DOG! BUT, READ ON... YOU'LL GET TO MEET THEM SOON ENOUGH...
DO YOU THINK SHE'LL REALLY BE OUT, AUNT SYLVIA?
OH-HO-HO! YOU COULD SET YOUR WATCH BY HER, FOUR O'CLOCK ON THE DOT.
PASS THOSE SCONES, CASS. YOU'RE SUCH A HOG. YOU MARRIED A HOG, HENRY. YOU KNOW THAT, DON'T YOU?
WILL WHO BE OUT, CASS?

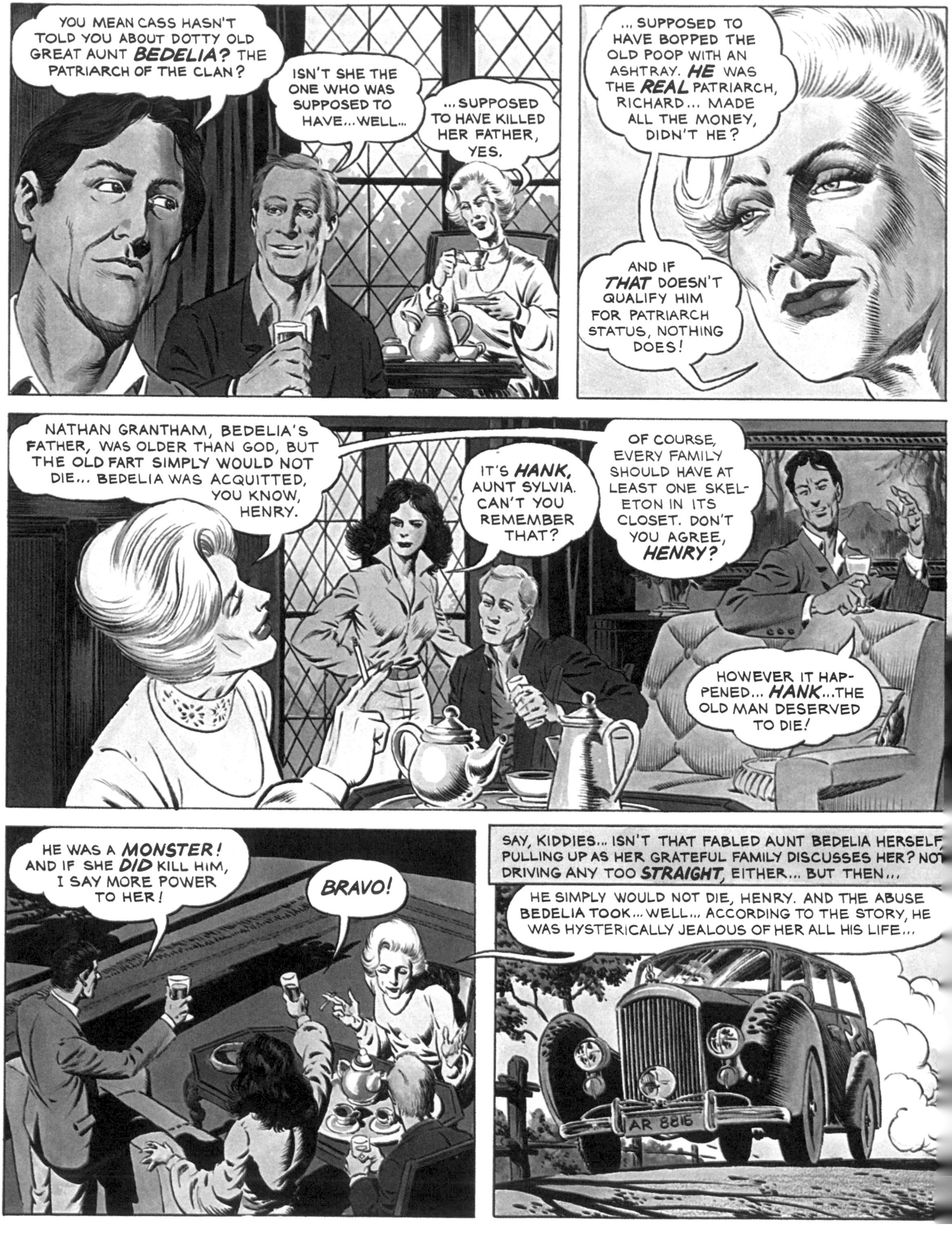
YOU MEAN CASS HASN'T TOLD YOU ABOUT DOTTY OLD GREAT AUNT BEDELIA? THE PATRIARCH OF THE CLAN?
ISN'T SHE THE ONE WHO WAS SUPPOSED TO HAVE...WELL...
...SUPPOSED TO HAVE KILLED HER FATHER, YES.
...SUPPOSED TO HAVE BOPPED THE OLD POOP WITH AN ASHTRAY. HE WAS THE REAL PATRIARCH, RICHARD... MADE ALL THE MONEY, DIDN'T HE?
AND IF THAT DOESN'T QUALIFY HIM FOR PATRIARCH STATUS, NOTHING DOES!
NATHAN GRANTHAM, BEDELIA'S FATHER, WAS OLDER THAN GOD, BUT THE OLD FART SIMPLY WOULD NOT DIE... BEDELIA WAS ACQUITTED, YOU KNOW, HENRY.
IT'S HANK, AUNT SYLVIA. CAN'T YOU REMEMBER THAT?
OF COURSE, EVERY FAMILY SHOULD HAVE AT LEAST ONE SKEL-ETON IN ITS CLOSET. DON'T YOU AGREE, HENRY?
HOWEVER IT HAP-PENED... HANK...THE OLD MAN DESERVED TO DIE!
HE WAS A MONSTER! AND IF SHE DID KILL HIM, I SAY MORE POWER TO HER!
BRAVO!
SAY, KIDDIES... ISN'T THAT FABLED AUNT BEDELIA HERSELF PULLING UP AS HER GRATEFUL FAMILY DISCUSSES HER? NOT DRIVING ANY TOO STRAIGHT, EITHER... BUT THEN...
HE SIMPLY WOULD NOT DIE, HENRY. AND THE ABUSE BEDELIA TOOK... WELL... ACCORDING TO THE STORY, HE WAS HYSTERICALLY JEALOUS OF HER ALL HIS LIFE...
AR 8816

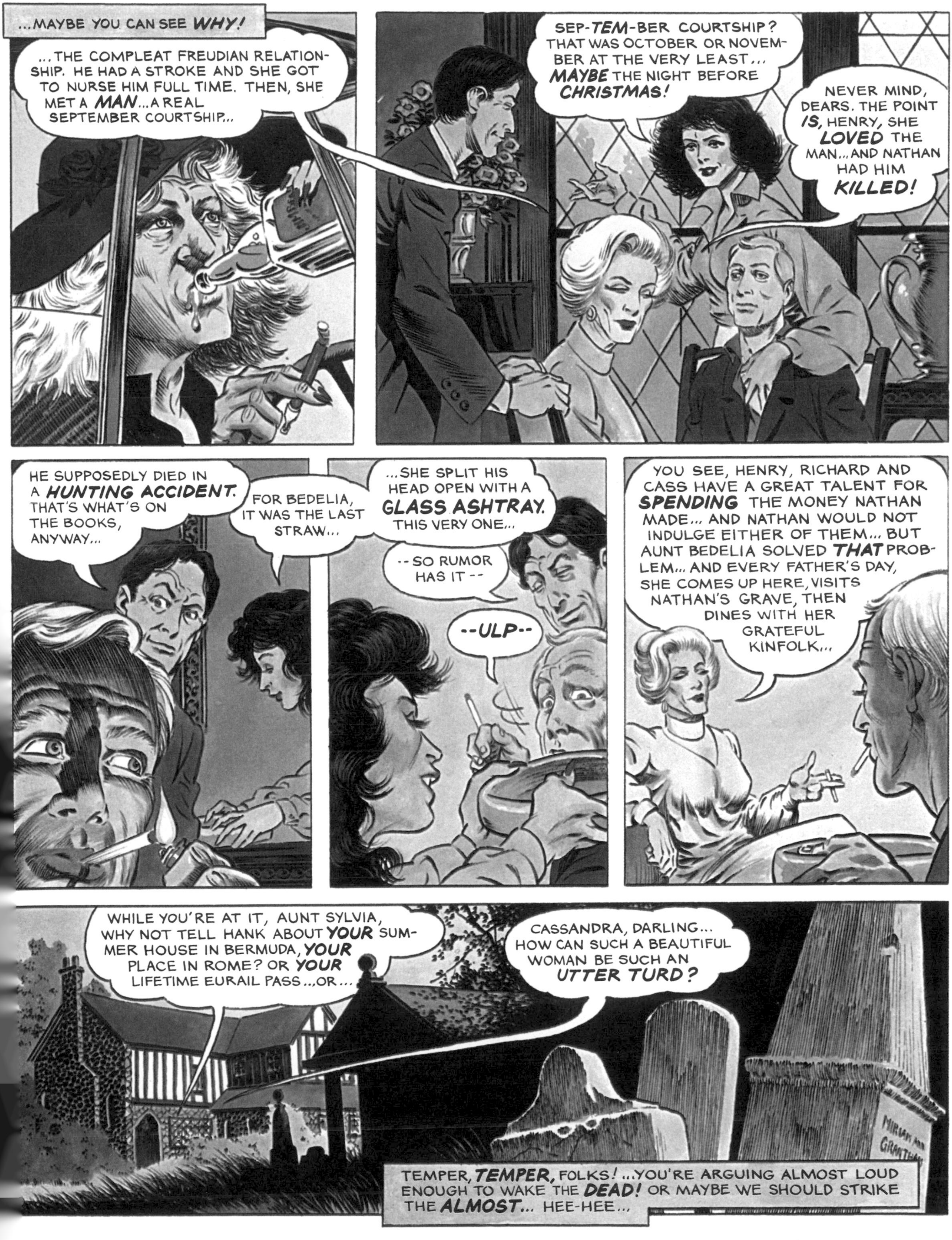
...MAYBE YOU CAN SEE WHY!
...THE COMPLEAT FREUDIAN RELATIONSHIP. HE HAD A STROKE AND SHE GOT TO NURSE HIM FULL TIME. THEN, SHE MET A MAN...A REAL SEPTEMBER COURTSHIP...
SEP-TEM-BER COURTSHIP? THAT WAS OCTOBER OR NOVEMBER AT THE VERY LEAST... MAYBE THE NIGHT BEFORE CHRISTMAS!
NEVER MIND, DEARS. THE POINT IS, HENRY, SHE LOVED THE MAN...AND NATHAN HAD HIM KILLED!
HE SUPPOSEDLY DIED IN A HUNTING ACCIDENT. THAT'S WHAT'S ON THE BOOKS, ANYWAY...
FOR BEDELIA, IT WAS THE LAST STRAW...
...SHE SPLIT HIS HEAD OPEN WITH A GLASS ASHTRAY. THIS VERY ONE...
--SO RUMOR HAS IT--
--ULP--
YOU SEE, HENRY, RICHARD AND CASS HAVE A GREAT TALENT FOR SPENDING THE MONEY NATHAN MADE... AND NATHAN WOULD NOT INDULGE EITHER OF THEM... BUT AUNT BEDELIA SOLVED THAT PROBLEM... AND EVERY FATHER'S DAY, SHE COMES UP HERE, VISITS NATHAN'S GRAVE, THEN DINES WITH HER GRATEFUL KINFOLK...
WHILE YOU'RE AT IT, AUNT SYLVIA, WHY NOT TELL HANK ABOUT YOUR SUMMER HOUSE IN BERMUDA, YOUR PLACE IN ROME? OR YOUR LIFETIME EURAIL PASS...,OR...
CASSANDRA, DARLING... HOW CAN SUCH A BEAUTIFUL WOMAN BE SUCH AN UTTER TURD?
TEMPER, TEMPER, FOLKS! ...YOU'RE ARGUING ALMOST LOUD ENOUGH TO WAKE THE DEAD! OR MAYBE WE SHOULD STRIKE THE ALMOST... HEE-HEE...

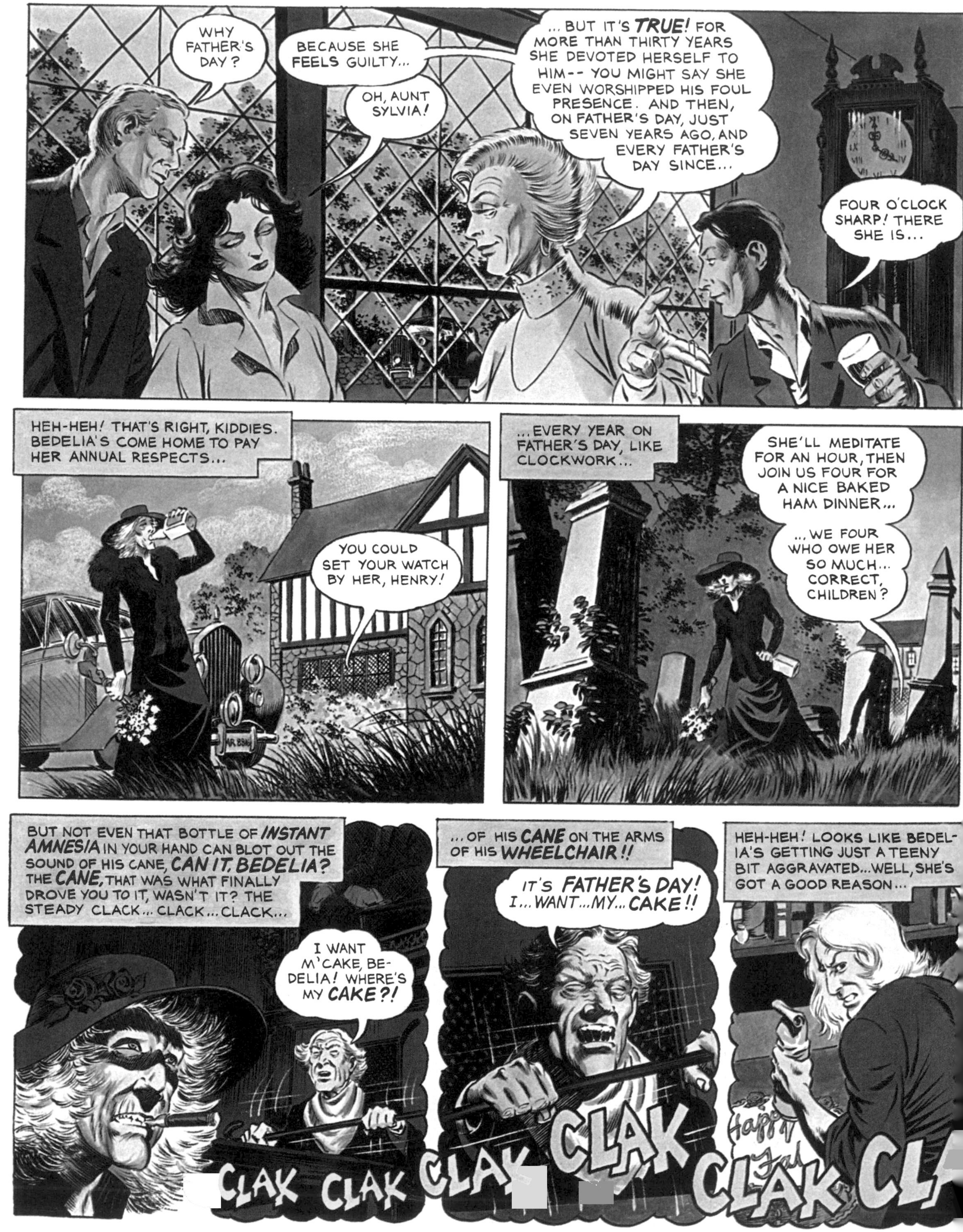
WHY FATHER'S DAY?
BECAUSE SHE FEELS GUILTY...
OH, AUNT SYLVIA!
... BUT IT'S TRUE! FOR MORE THAN THIRTY YEARS SHE DEVOTED HERSELF TO HIM-- YOU MIGHT SAY SHE EVEN WORSHIPPED HIS FOUL PRESENCE. AND THEN, ON FATHER'S DAY, JUST SEVEN YEARS AGO, AND EVERY FATHER'S DAY SINCE...
FOUR O'CLOCK SHARP! THERE SHE IS...
HEH-HEH! THAT'S RIGHT, KIDDIES. BEDELIA'S COME HOME TO PAY HER ANNUAL RESPECTS...
YOU COULD SET YOUR WATCH BY HER, HENRY!
...EVERY YEAR ON FATHER'S DAY, LIKE CLOCKWORK...
SHE'LL MEDITATE FOR AN HOUR, THEN JOIN US FOUR FOR A NICE BAKED HAM DINNER...
...WE FOUR WHO OWE HER SO MUCH... CORRECT, CHILDREN?
BUT NOT EVEN THAT BOTTLE OF INSTANT AMNESIA IN YOUR HAND CAN BLOT OUT THE SOUND OF HIS CANE, CAN IT, BEDELIA? THE CANE, THAT WAS WHAT FINALLY DROVE YOU TO IT, WASN'T IT? THE STEADY CLACK... CLACK... CLACK...
I WANT M'CAKE, BEDELIA! WHERE'S MY CAKE?!
CLAK CLAK CLAK
...OF HIS CANE ON THE ARMS OF HIS WHEELCHAIR!!
IT'S FATHER'S DAY! I... WANT... MY... CAKE!!
CLAK
HEH-HEH! LOOKS LIKE BEDELIA'S GETTING JUST A TEENY BIT AGGRAVATED... WELL, SHE'S GOT A GOOD REASON...
CLAK CL

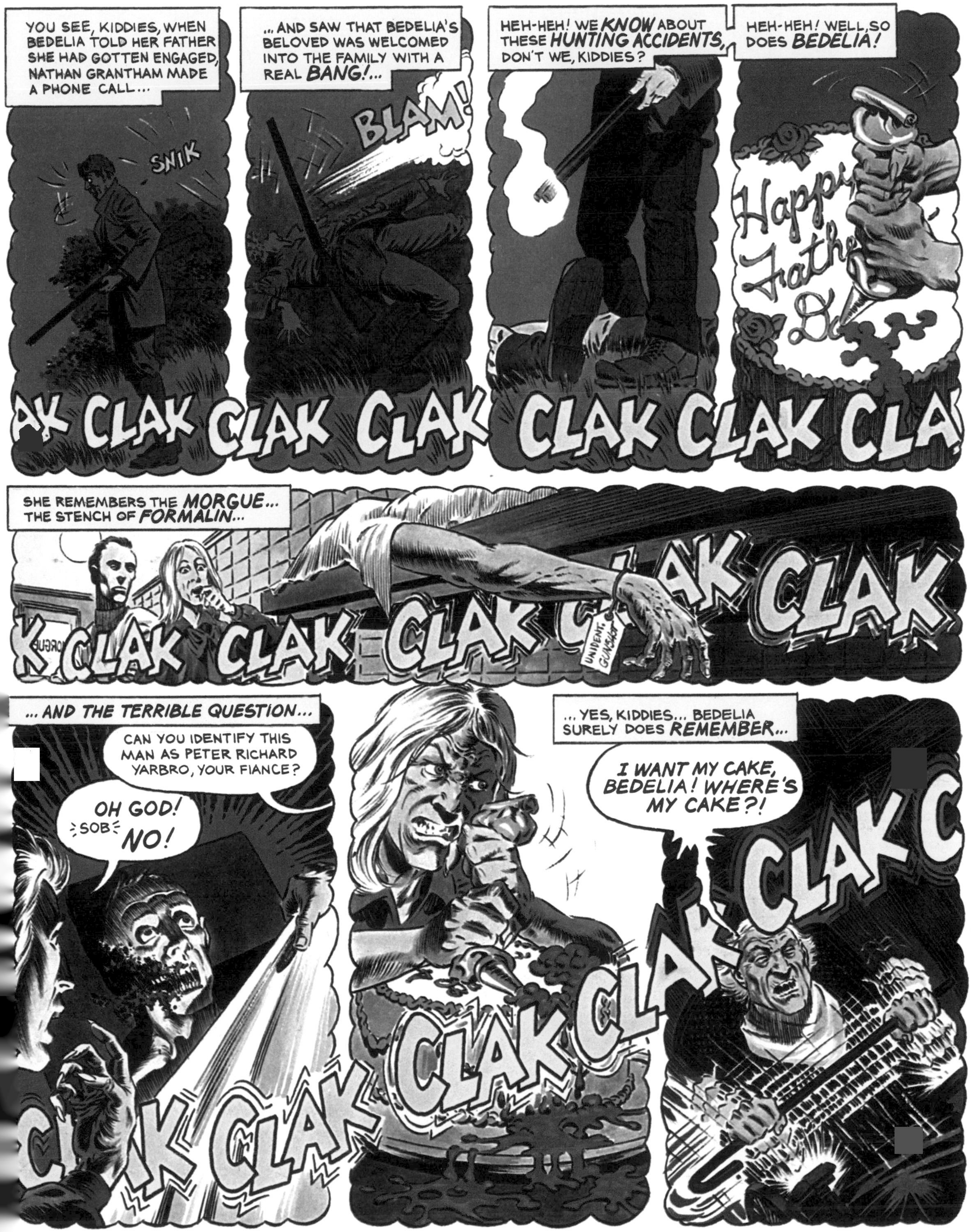

YOU SEE, KIDDIES, WHEN BEDELIA TOLD HER FATHER SHE HAD GOTTEN ENGAGED, NATHAN GRANTHAM MADE A PHONE CALL...
SNIK
...AND SAW THAT BEDELIA'S BELOVED WAS WELCOMED INTO THE FAMILY WITH A REAL BANG!...
BLAM!
HEH-HEH! WE KNOW ABOUT THESE HUNTING ACCIDENTS, DON'T WE, KIDDIES?
HEH-HEH! WELL, SO DOES BEDELIA!
Happy Fathe Da
AK CLAK CLAK CLAK CLAK CLAK CLA
SHE REMEMBERS THE MORGUE... THE STENCH OF FORMALIN...
K CLAK CLAK CLAK CLAK CLAK
UNIDENT. GUNSHOT
...AND THE TERRIBLE QUESTION...
CAN YOU IDENTIFY THIS MAN AS PETER RICHARD YARBRO, YOUR FIANCE?
OH GOD! SOB NO!
...YES, KIDDIES... BEDELIA SURELY DOES REMEMBER...
I WANT MY CAKE, BEDELIA! WHERE'S MY CAKE?!
CLAK CLAK CLAK CLAK CLAK CLAK C

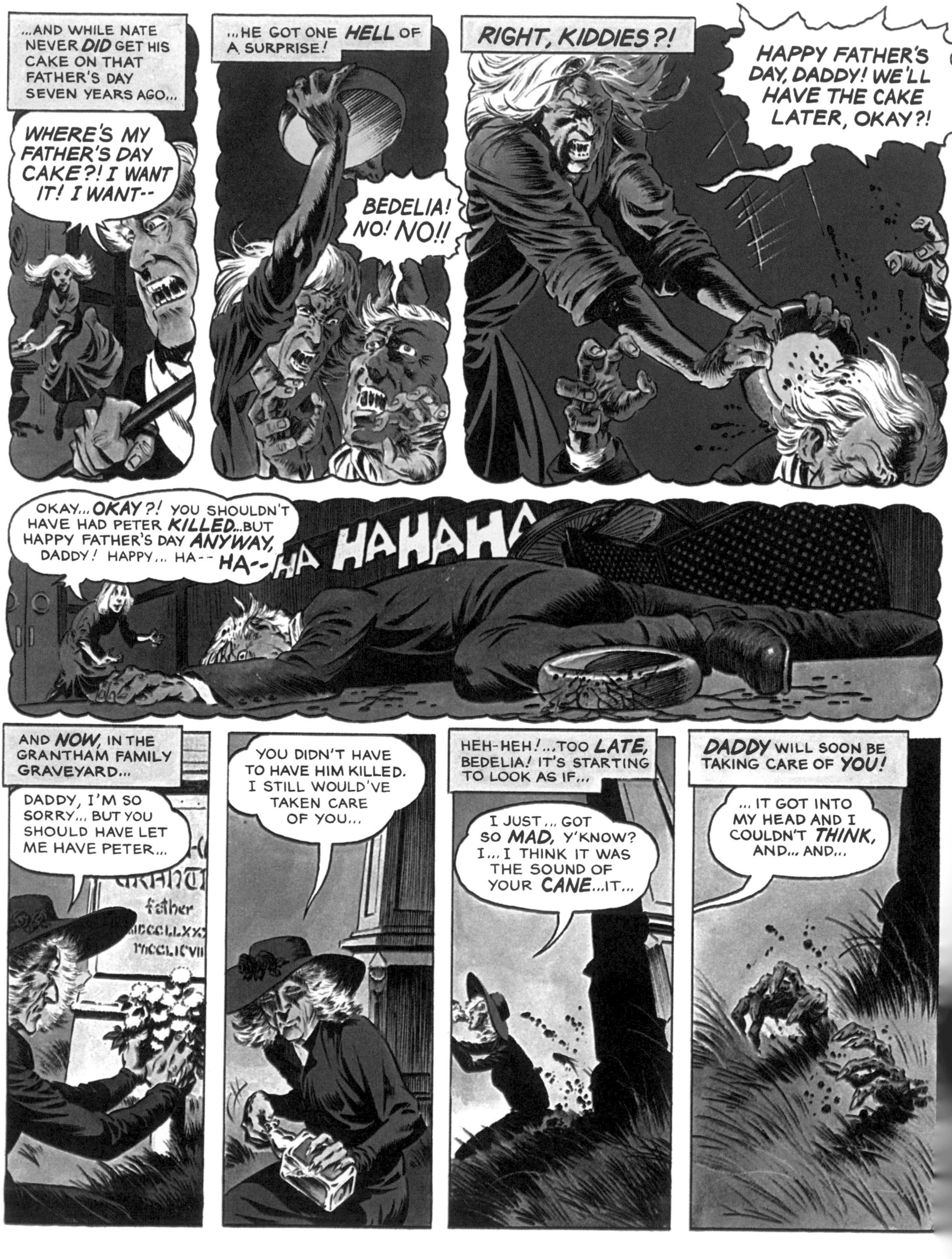

...AND WHILE NATE NEVER DID GET HIS CAKE ON THAT FATHER'S DAY SEVEN YEARS AGO...
WHERE'S MY FATHER'S DAY CAKE?! I WANT IT! I WANT--
...HE GOT ONE HELL OF A SURPRISE!
BEDELIA! NO! NO!!
RIGHT, KIDDIES?!
HAPPY FATHER'S DAY, DADDY! WE'LL HAVE THE CAKE LATER, OKAY?!
OKAY... OKAY?! YOU SHOULDN'T HAVE HAD PETER KILLED...BUT HAPPY FATHER'S DAY ANYWAY, DADDY! HAPPY... HA-- HA--
HA HAHAHA
AND NOW, IN THE GRANTHAM FAMILY GRAVEYARD...
DADDY, I'M SO SORRY... BUT YOU SHOULD HAVE LET ME HAVE PETER...
father
YOU DIDN'T HAVE TO HAVE HIM KILLED. I STILL WOULD'VE TAKEN CARE OF YOU...
HEH-HEH!...TOO LATE, BEDELIA! IT'S STARTING TO LOOK AS IF...
I JUST... GOT SO MAD, Y'KNOW? I... I THINK IT WAS THE SOUND OF YOUR CANE...IT...
DADDY WILL SOON BE TAKING CARE OF YOU!
... IT GOT INTO MY HEAD AND I COULDN'T THINK, AND... AND...

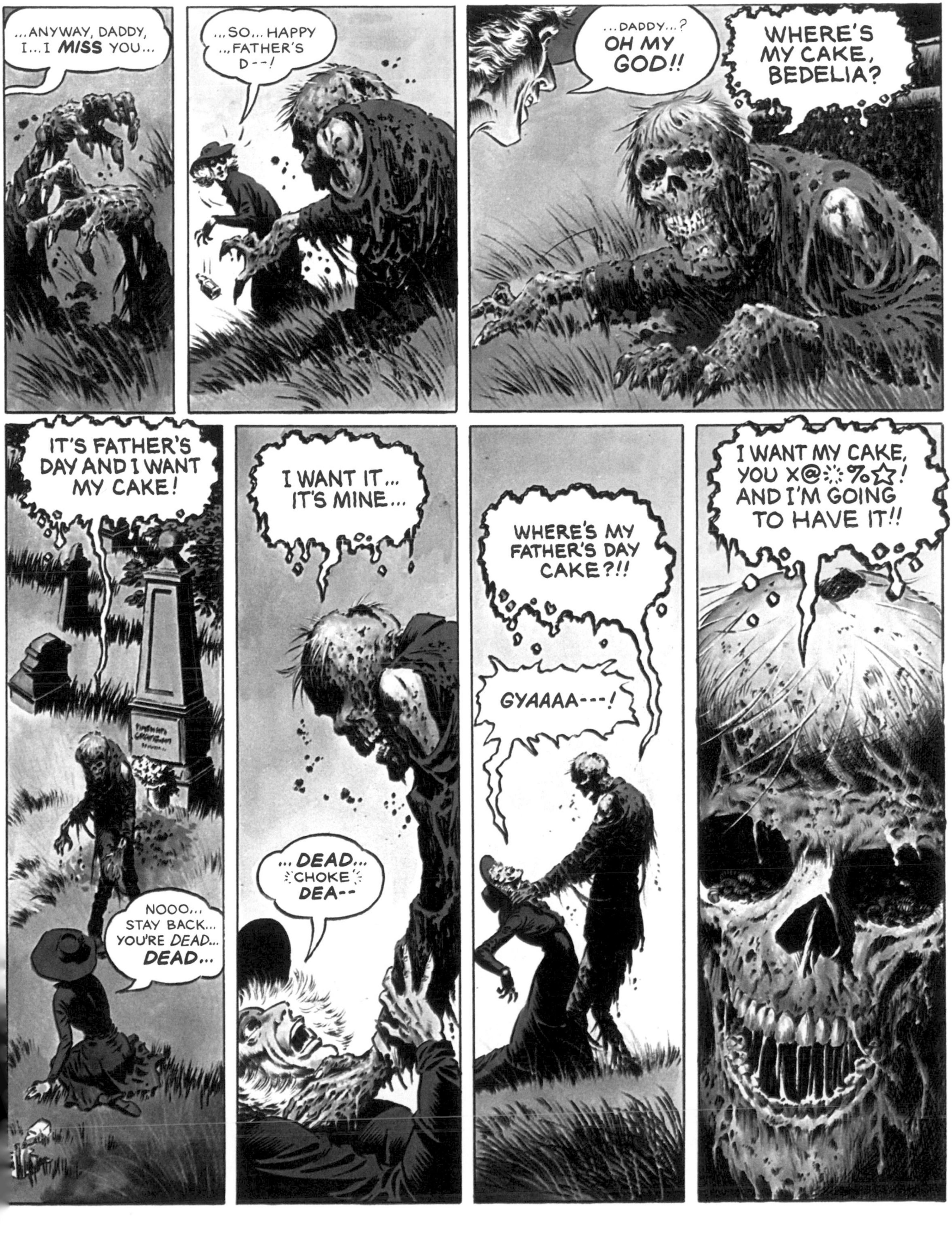
...ANYWAY, DADDY, I...I MISS YOU...
...SO...HAPPY ...FATHER'S D--!
...DADDY...? OH MY GOD!!
WHERE'S MY CAKE, BEDELIA?
IT'S FATHER'S DAY AND I WANT MY CAKE!
NOOO,.. STAY BACK... YOU'RE DEAD... DEAD...
I WANT IT... IT'S MINE...
...DEAD... CHOKE DEA--
WHERE'S MY FATHER'S DAY CAKE?!!
GYAAAA---!
I WANT MY CAKE, YOU X@*%☆! AND I'M GOING TO HAVE IT!!

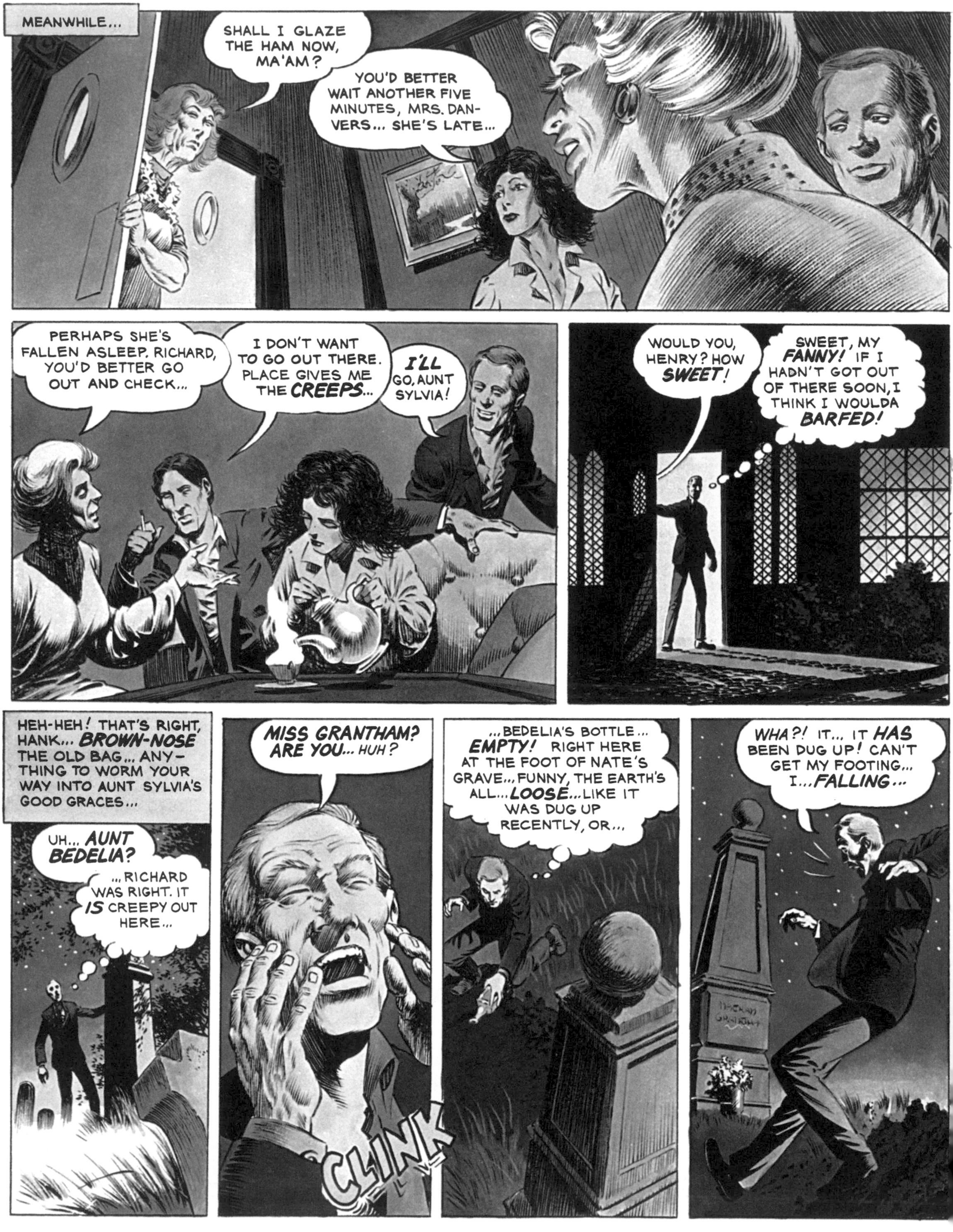
MEANWHILE...
SHALL I GLAZE THE HAM NOW, MA'AM?
YOU'D BETTER WAIT ANOTHER FIVE MINUTES, MRS. DANVERS... SHE'S LATE...
PERHAPS SHE'S FALLEN ASLEEP, RICHARD, YOU'D BETTER GO OUT AND CHECK...
I DON'T WANT TO GO OUT THERE. PLACE GIVES ME THE CREEPS...
I'LL GO, AUNT SYLVIA!
WOULD YOU, HENRY? HOW SWEET!
SWEET, MY FANNY! IF I HADN'T GOT OUT OF THERE SOON, I THINK I WOULDA BARFED!
HEH-HEH! THAT'S RIGHT, HANK... BROWN-NOSE THE OLD BAG... ANYTHING TO WORM YOUR WAY INTO AUNT SYLVIA'S GOOD GRACES...
UH... AUNT BEDELIA?
...RICHARD WAS RIGHT. IT IS CREEPY OUT HERE...
MISS GRANTHAM? ARE YOU... HUH?
CLINK
...BEDELIA'S BOTTLE... EMPTY! RIGHT HERE AT THE FOOT OF NATE'S GRAVE... FUNNY, THE EARTH'S ALL... LOOSE... LIKE IT WAS DUG UP RECENTLY, OR...
WHA?! IT... IT HAS BEEN DUG UP! CAN'T GET MY FOOTING... I... FALLING...

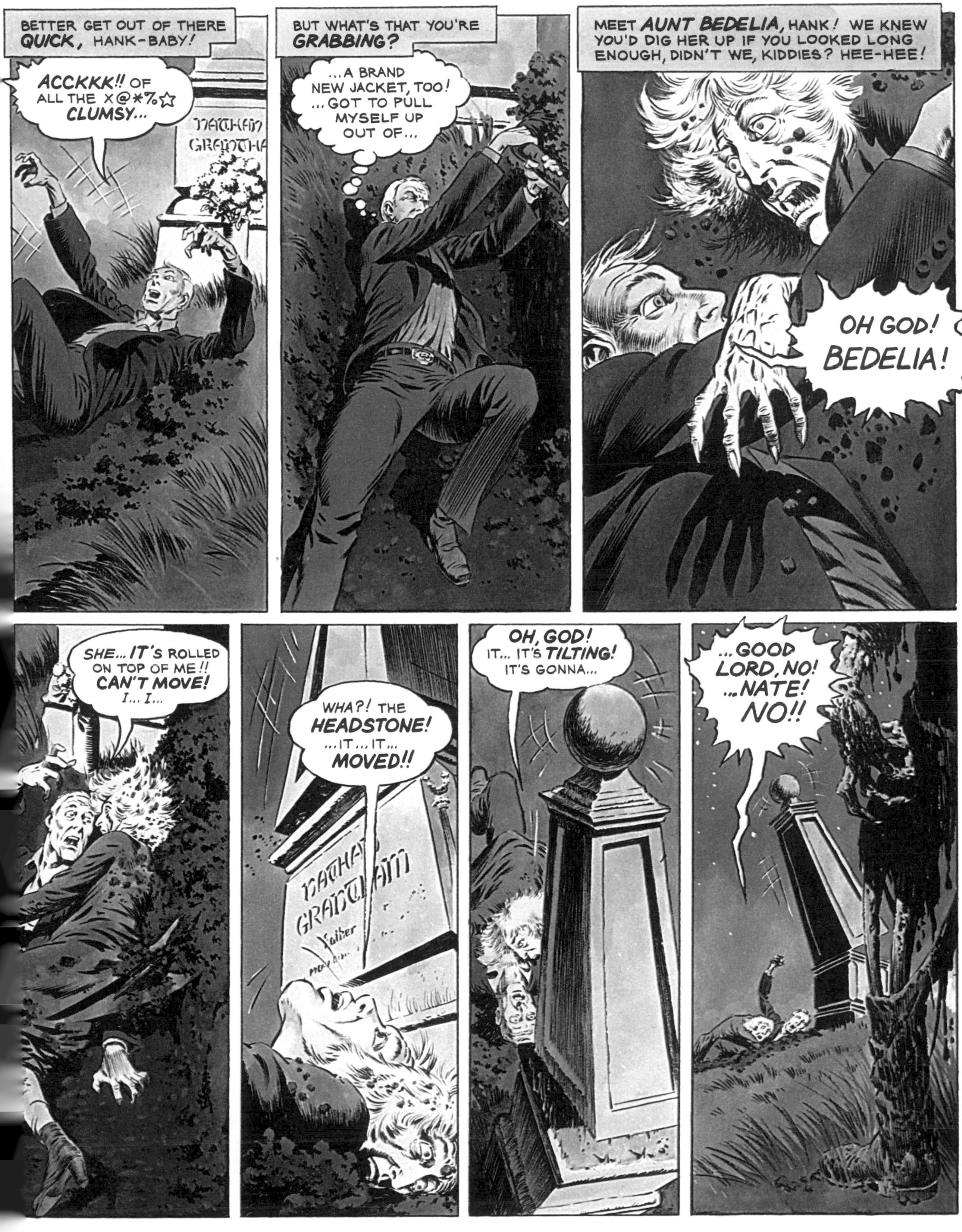

BETTER GET OUT OF THERE QUICK, HANK-BABY!
ACCKKK!! OF ALL THE X@*%☆ CLUMSY...
NATHAN GRANTHA
BUT WHAT'S THAT YOU'RE GRABBING?
...A BRAND NEW JACKET, TOO! ...GOT TO PULL MYSELF UP OUT OF...
MEET AUNT BEDELIA, HANK! WE KNEW YOU'D DIG HER UP IF YOU LOOKED LONG ENOUGH, DIDN'T WE, KIDDIES? HEE-HEE!
OH GOD! BEDELIA!
SHE... IT'S ROLLED ON TOP OF ME!! CAN'T MOVE! I... I...
WHA?! THE HEADSTONE! ...IT... IT... MOVED!!
NATHAN GRANTHAM
Father
OH, GOD! IT... IT'S TILTING! IT'S GONNA...
...GOOD LORD, NO! ...NATE! NO!!

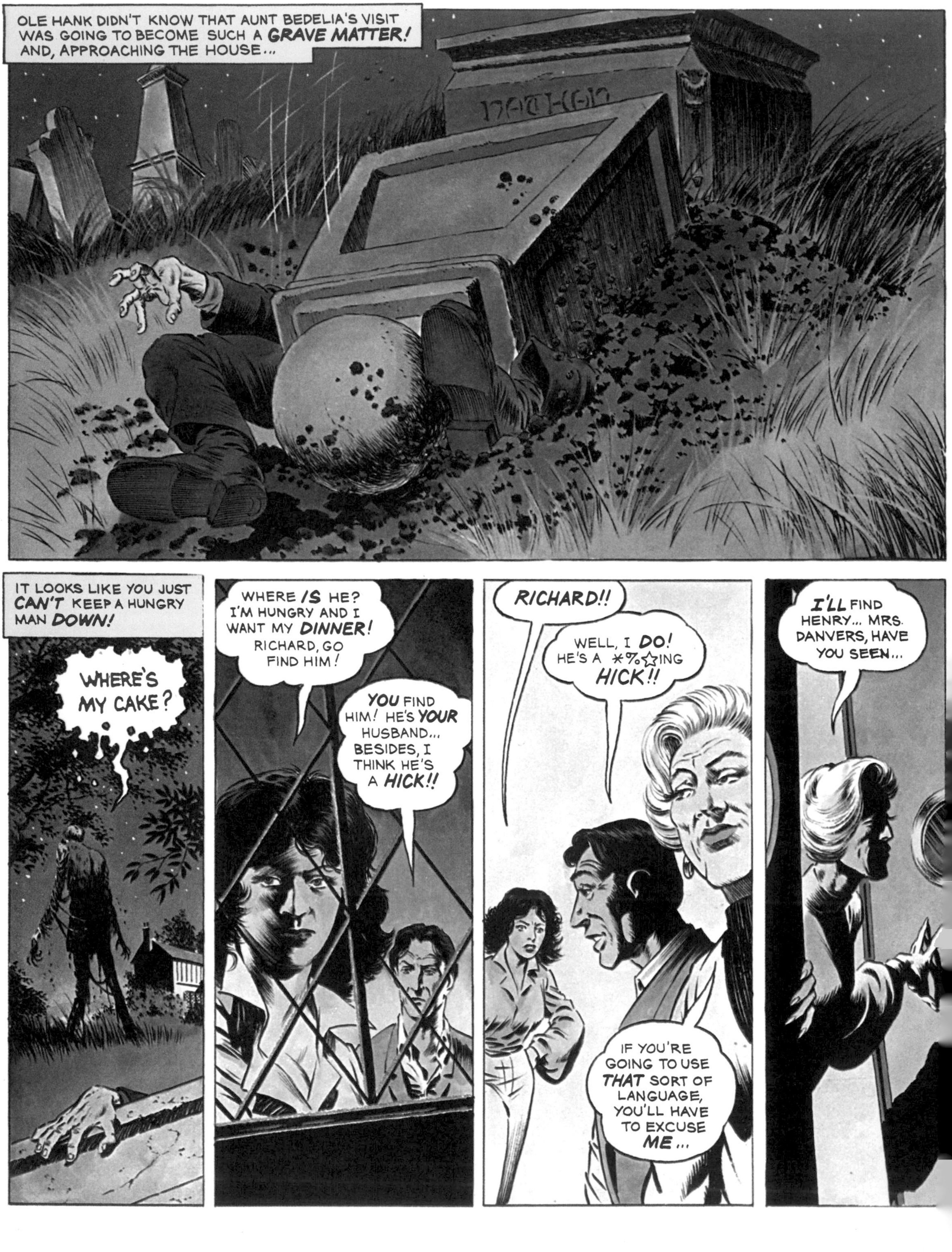

OLE HANK DIDN'T KNOW THAT AUNT BEDELIA'S VISIT WAS GOING TO BECOME SUCH A GRAVE MATTER! AND, APPROACHING THE HOUSE...
IT LOOKS LIKE YOU JUST CAN'T KEEP A HUNGRY MAN DOWN!
WHERE'S MY CAKE?
WHERE IS HE? I'M HUNGRY AND I WANT MY DINNER! RICHARD, GO FIND HIM!
YOU FIND HIM! HE'S YOUR HUSBAND... BESIDES, I THINK HE'S A HICK!!
RICHARD!!
WELL, I DO! HE'S A *%☆ING HICK!!
IF YOU'RE GOING TO USE THAT SORT OF LANGUAGE, YOU'LL HAVE TO EXCUSE ME...
I'LL FIND HENRY... MRS. DANVERS, HAVE YOU SEEN...

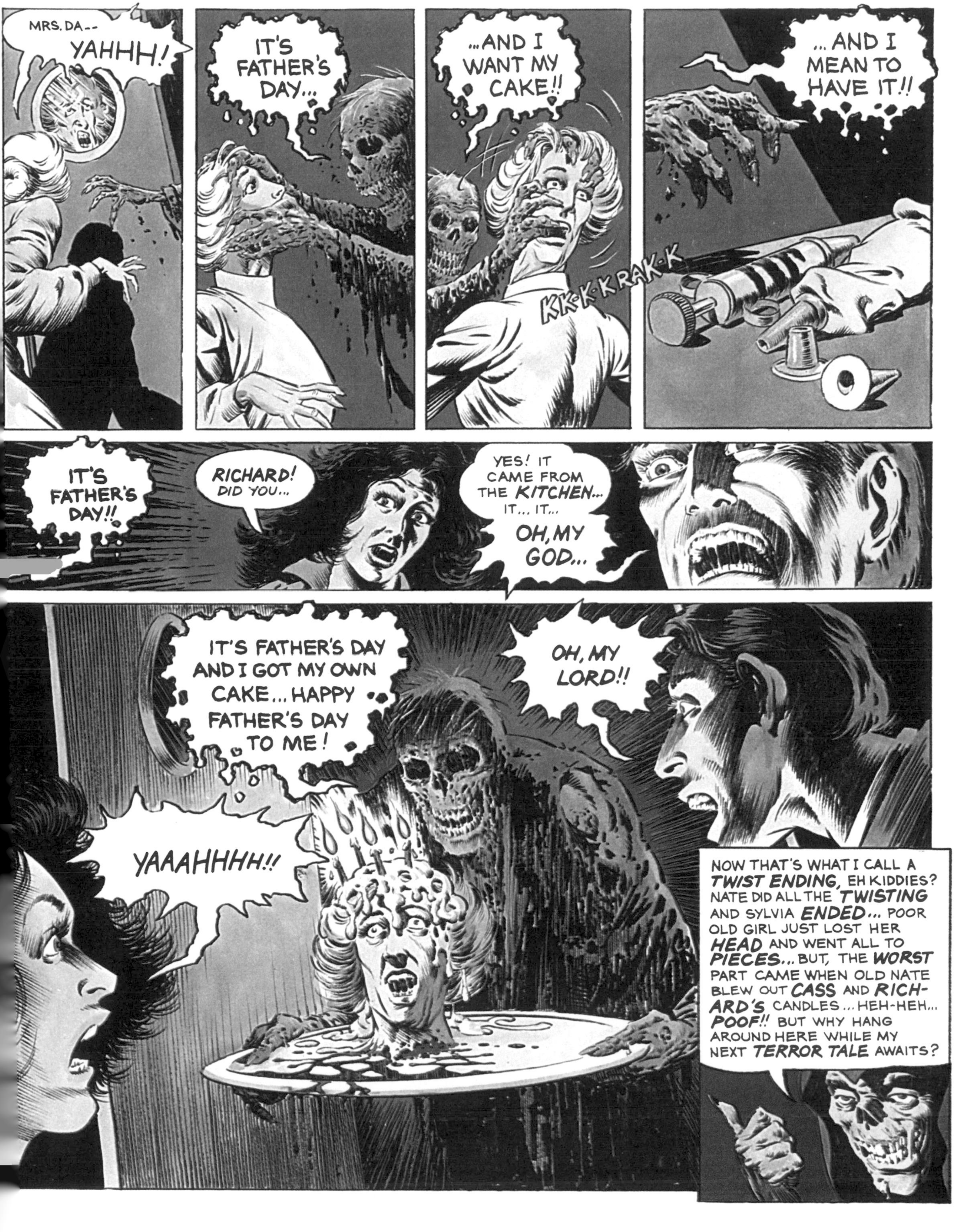
MRS. DA--
YAHHH!
IT'S FATHER'S DAY...
...AND I WANT MY CAKE!!
...AND I MEAN TO HAVE IT!!
KK-K-K RAK-K-K
IT'S FATHER'S DAY!!
RICHARD! DID YOU...
YES! IT CAME FROM THE KITCHEN... IT... IT...
OH, MY GOD...
IT'S FATHER'S DAY AND I GOT MY OWN CAKE... HAPPY FATHER'S DAY TO ME!
OH, MY LORD!!
YAAAHHHH!!
NOW THAT'S WHAT I CALL A TWIST ENDING, EH KIDDIES? NATE DID ALL THE TWISTING AND SYLVIA ENDED... POOR OLD GIRL JUST LOST HER HEAD AND WENT ALL TO PIECES... BUT, THE WORST PART CAME WHEN OLD NATE BLEW OUT CASS AND RICHARD'S CANDLES... HEH-HEH... POOF!! BUT WHY HANG AROUND HERE WHILE MY NEXT TERROR TALE AWAITS?

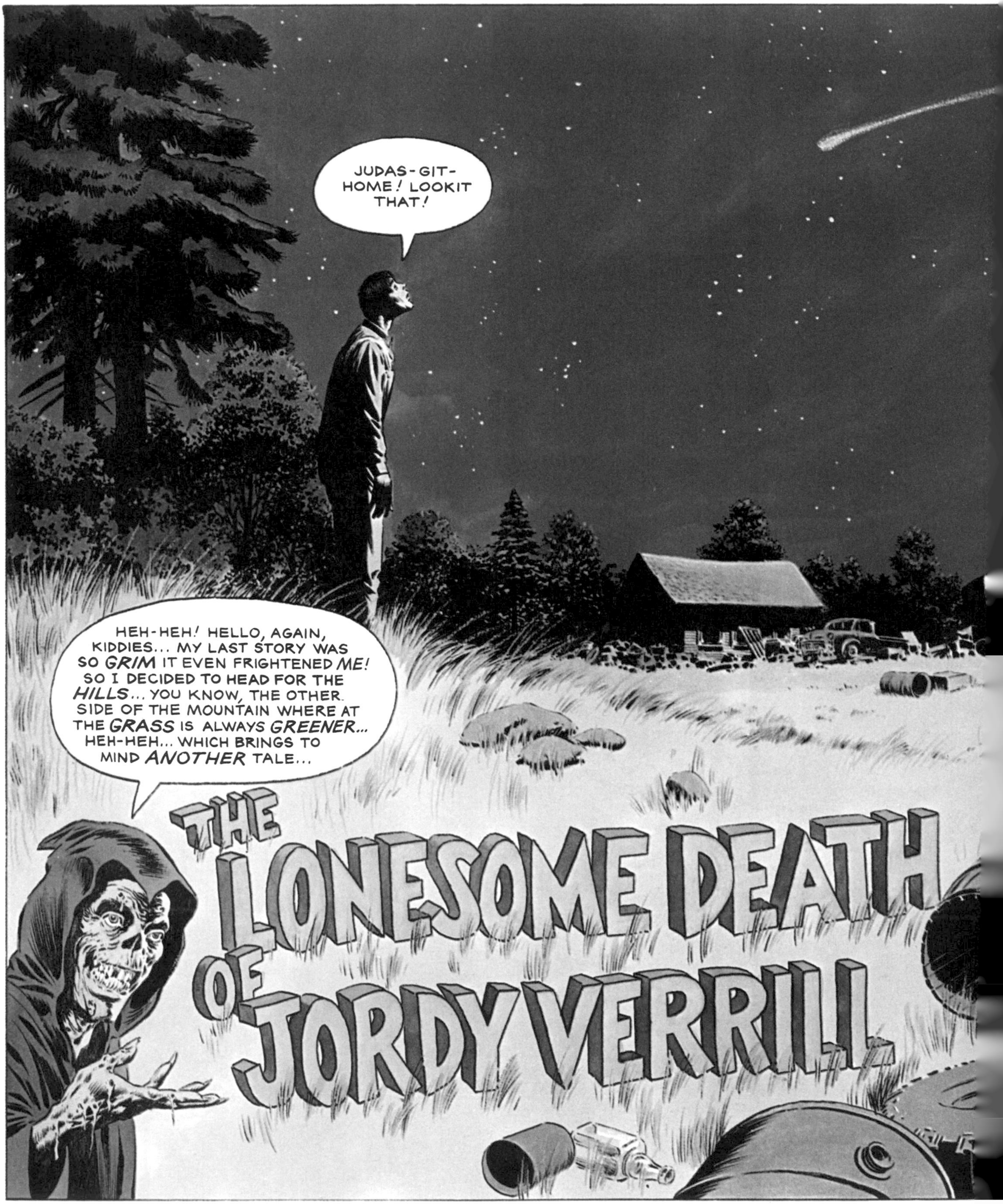
JUDAS-GIT-HOME! LOOKIT THAT!
HEH-HEH! HELLO, AGAIN, KIDDIES... MY LAST STORY WAS SO GRIM IT EVEN FRIGHTENED ME! SO I DECIDED TO HEAD FOR THE HILLS... YOU KNOW, THE OTHER SIDE OF THE MOUNTAIN WHERE AT THE GRASS IS ALWAYS GREENER... HEH-HEH... WHICH BRINGS TO MIND ANOTHER TALE...
THE LONESOME DEATH OF JORDY VERRILL

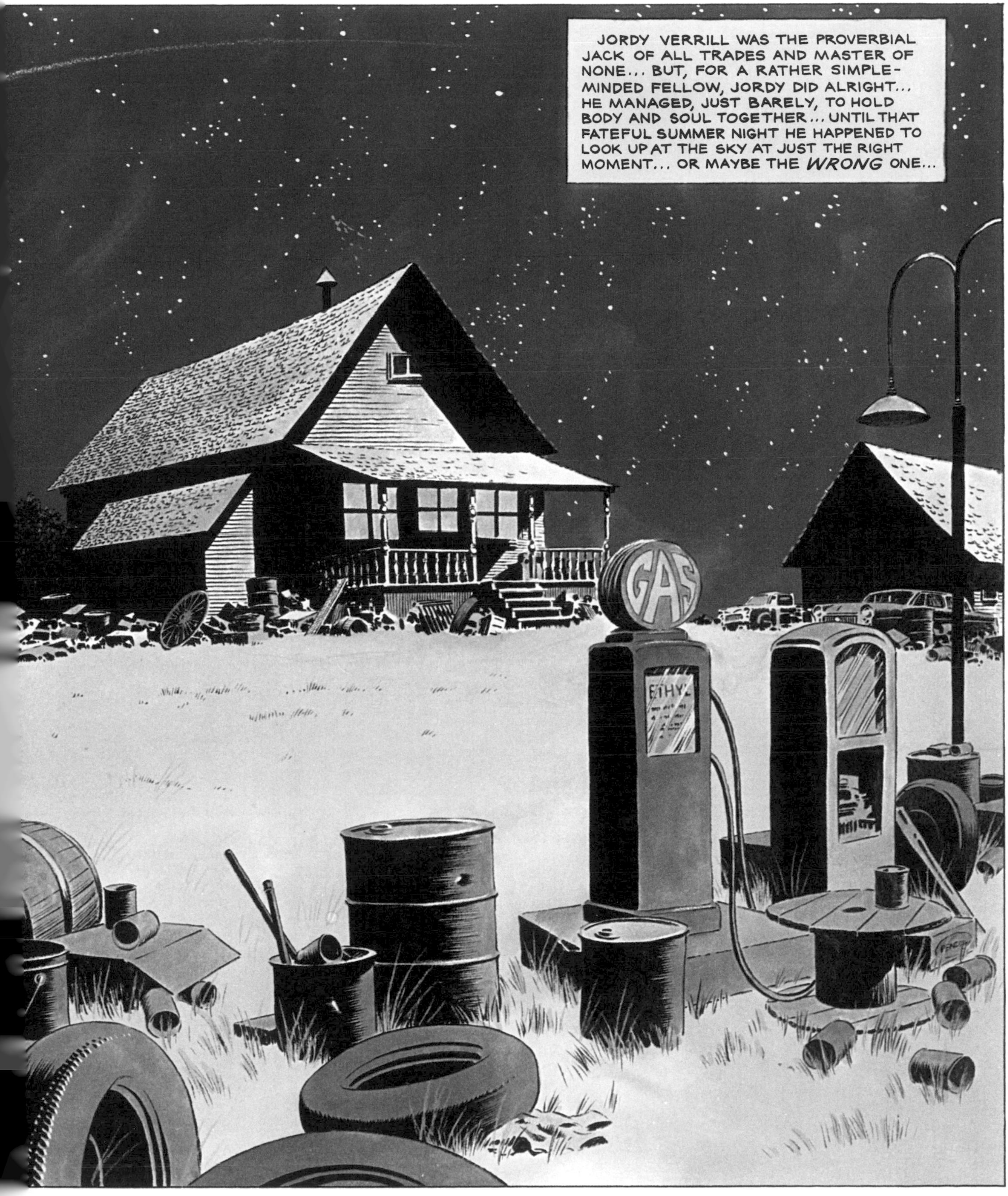
JORDY VERRILL WAS THE PROVERBIAL JACK OF ALL TRADES AND MASTER OF NONE... BUT, FOR A RATHER SIMPLE-MINDED FELLOW, JORDY DID ALRIGHT... HE MANAGED, JUST BARELY, TO HOLD BODY AND SOUL TOGETHER... UNTIL THAT FATEFUL SUMMER NIGHT HE HAPPENED TO LOOK UP AT THE SKY AT JUST THE RIGHT MOMENT... OR MAYBE THE *WRONG* ONE...
GAS
ETHYL

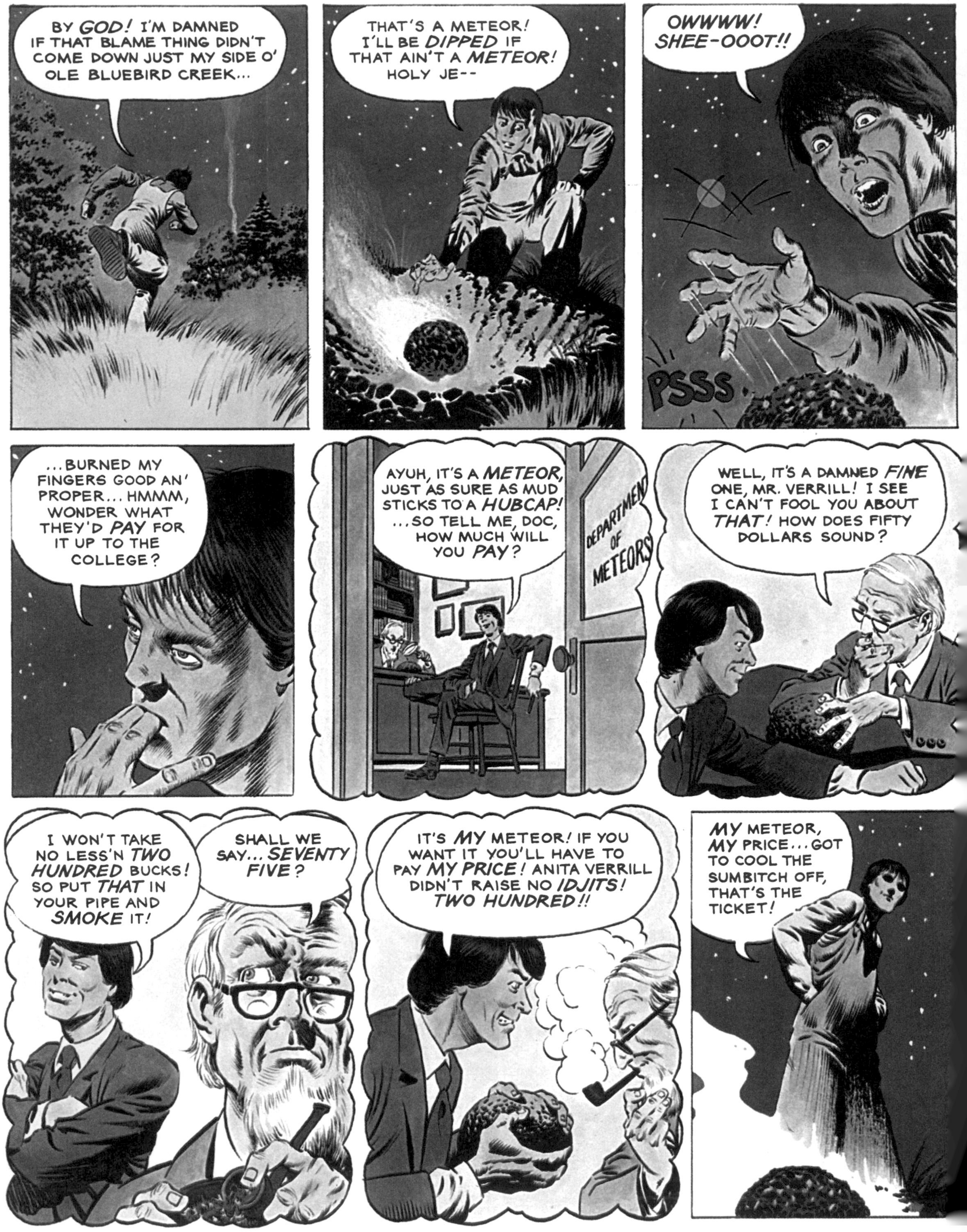

BY GOD! I'M DAMNED IF THAT BLAME THING DIDN'T COME DOWN JUST MY SIDE O' OLE BLUEBIRD CREEK...
THAT'S A METEOR! I'LL BE DIPPED IF THAT AIN'T A METEOR! HOLY JE--
OWWWW! SHEE-OOOT!!
PSSS
...BURNED MY FINGERS GOOD AN' PROPER... HMMM, WONDER WHAT THEY'D PAY FOR IT UP TO THE COLLEGE?
AYUH, IT'S A METEOR, JUST AS SURE AS MUD STICKS TO A HUBCAP! ...SO TELL ME, DOC, HOW MUCH WILL YOU PAY?
DEPARTMENT OF METEORS
WELL, IT'S A DAMNED FINE ONE, MR. VERRILL! I SEE I CAN'T FOOL YOU ABOUT THAT! HOW DOES FIFTY DOLLARS SOUND?
I WON'T TAKE NO LESS'N TWO HUNDRED BUCKS! SO PUT THAT IN YOUR PIPE AND SMOKE IT!
SHALL WE SAY... SEVENTY FIVE?
IT'S MY METEOR! IF YOU WANT IT YOU'LL HAVE TO PAY MY PRICE! ANITA VERRILL DIDN'T RAISE NO IDJITS! TWO HUNDRED!!
MY METEOR, MY PRICE... GOT TO COOL THE SUMBITCH OFF, THAT'S THE TICKET!

BUCKET OR TWO OF WATER'LL DO THE TRICK! I...OWWW!

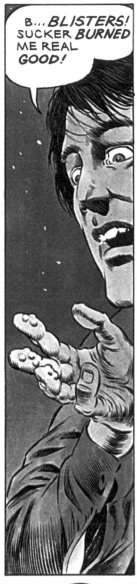

B...BLISTERS! SUCKER BURNED ME REAL GOOD!

WELL, NO MATTER...

...CAUSE THIS TIME OLE JORDY...

...HAS GOT IT MADE!!

SSSSSSSSS

I'M SORRY, MR. VERRILL...WE SIMPLY CAN'T CARRY YOUR LOAN ANY LONGER. I'M AFRAID WE'LL HAVE TO...

YOU WON'T HAVE TO, MR. BILKMORE!

WOULD YOU MIND TELLING ME, MR. VERRILL, JUST HOW YOU CAME BY THIS MONEY?

YOU MIGHT SAY IT FELL OUT OF THE SKY!!

...OUT OF THE SKY! HAW-HAW! THAT'S...

HUH?

SSSCRACKSSS

THE...THE WATER WAS TOO COLD! CRACKED THE METEOR WIDE OPEN! OH, YOU DONE IT NOW, JORDY VERRILL, YOU LUNKHEAD!

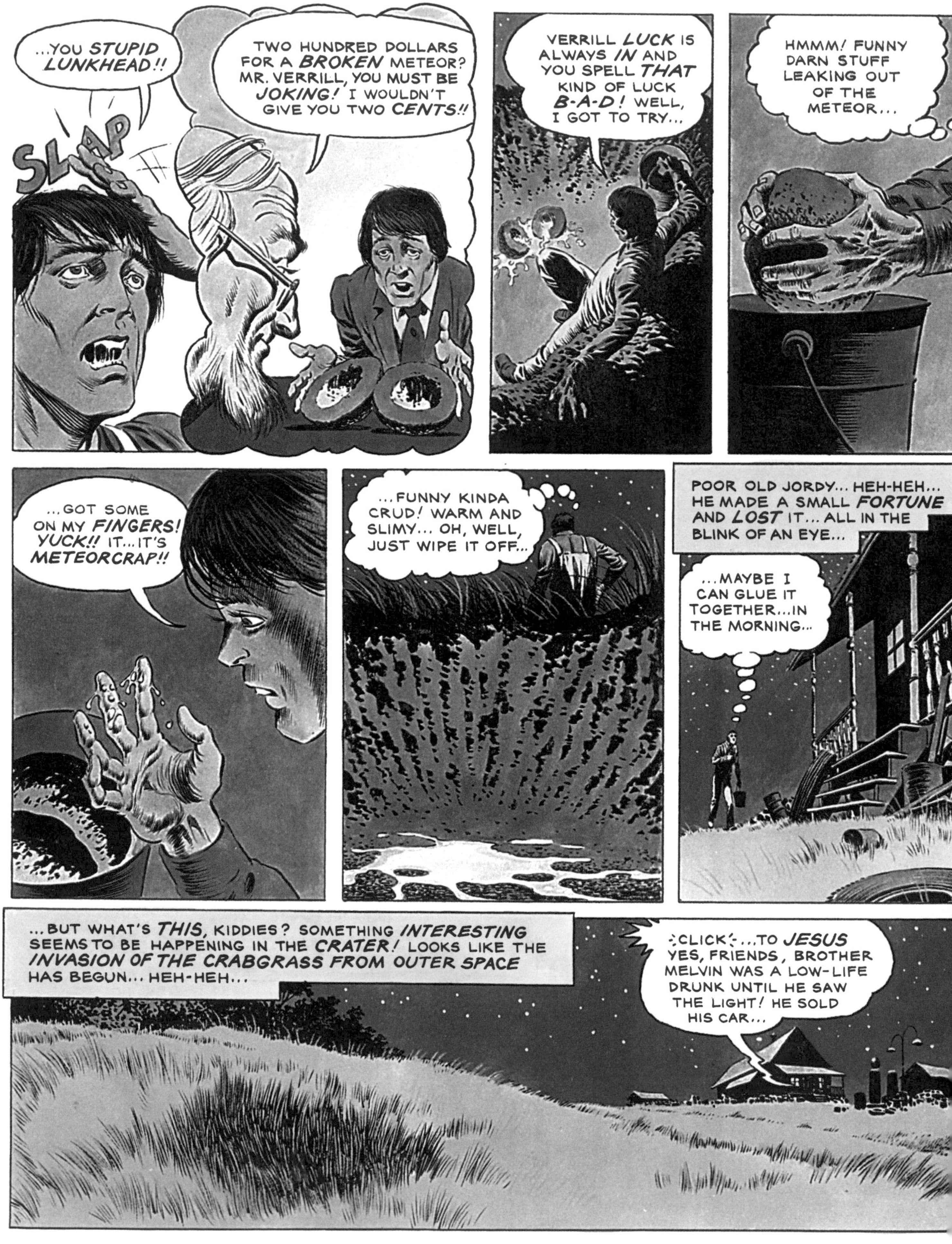
...YOU STUPID LUNKHEAD!!
SLAP
TWO HUNDRED DOLLARS FOR A BROKEN METEOR? MR. VERRILL, YOU MUST BE JOKING! I WOULDN'T GIVE YOU TWO CENTS!!
VERRILL LUCK IS ALWAYS IN AND YOU SPELL THAT KIND OF LUCK B-A-D! WELL, I GOT TO TRY...
HMMM! FUNNY DARN STUFF LEAKING OUT OF THE METEOR...
...GOT SOME ON MY FINGERS! YUCK!! IT...IT'S METEORCRAP!!
...FUNNY KINDA CRUD! WARM AND SLIMY... OH, WELL, JUST WIPE IT OFF...
POOR OLD JORDY... HEH-HEH... HE MADE A SMALL FORTUNE AND LOST IT... ALL IN THE BLINK OF AN EYE...
...MAYBE I CAN GLUE IT TOGETHER...IN THE MORNING...
...BUT WHAT'S THIS, KIDDIES? SOMETHING INTERESTING SEEMS TO BE HAPPENING IN THE CRATER! LOOKS LIKE THE INVASION OF THE CRABGRASS FROM OUTER SPACE HAS BEGUN... HEH-HEH...
-CLICK-...TO JESUS YES, FRIENDS, BROTHER MELVIN WAS A LOW-LIFE DRUNK UNTIL HE SAW THE LIGHT! HE SOLD HIS CAR...

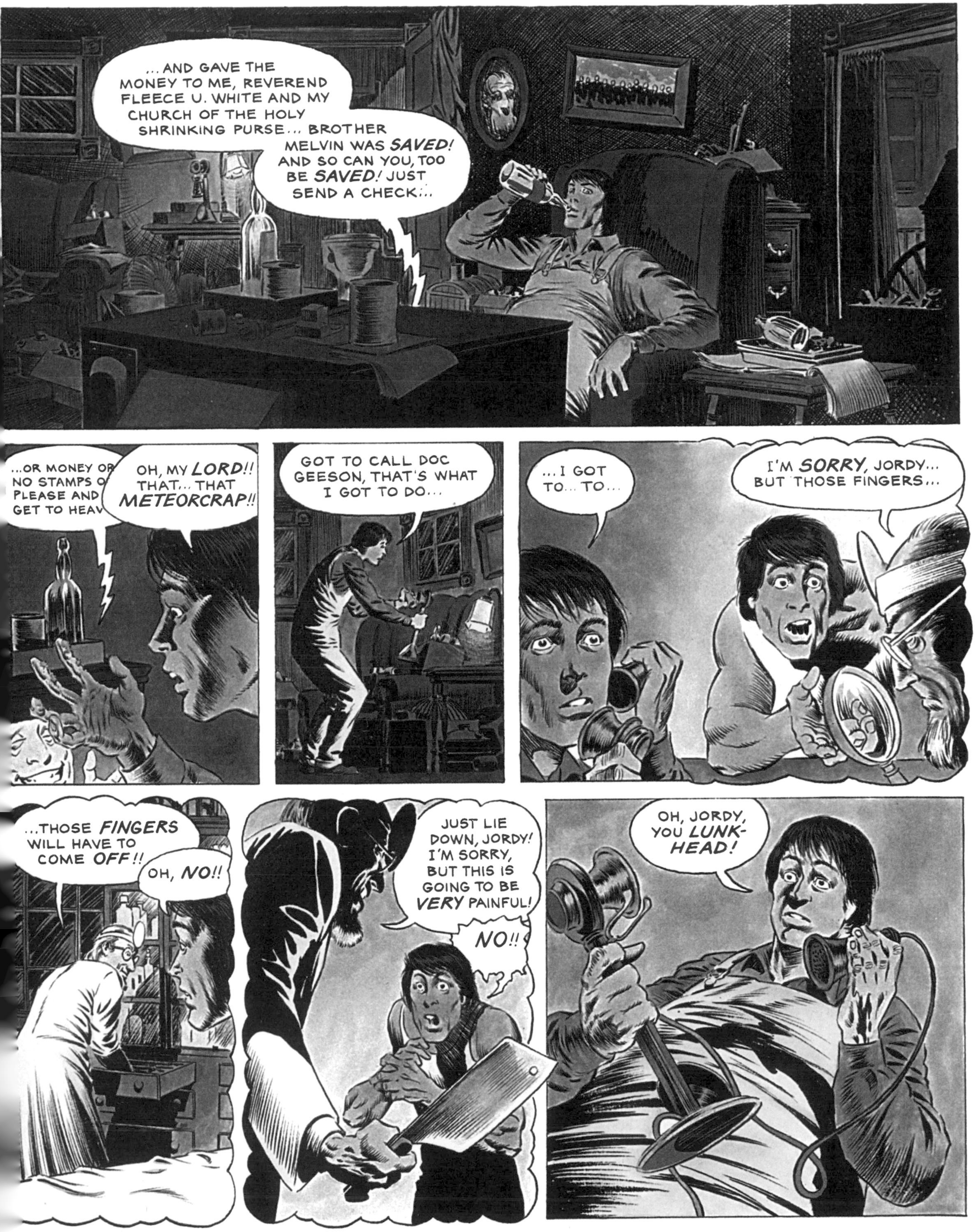
...AND GAVE THE MONEY TO ME, REVEREND FLEECE U. WHITE AND MY CHURCH OF THE HOLY SHRINKING PURSE... BROTHER MELVIN WAS SAVED! AND SO CAN YOU, TOO BE SAVED! JUST SEND A CHECK...
...OR MONEY OR NO STAMPS O PLEASE AND GET TO HEAV
OH, MY LORD!! THAT... THAT METEORCRAP!!
GOT TO CALL DOC GEESON, THAT'S WHAT I GOT TO DO...
...I GOT TO... TO...
I'M SORRY, JORDY... BUT THOSE FINGERS...
...THOSE FINGERS WILL HAVE TO COME OFF!!
OH, NO!!
JUST LIE DOWN, JORDY! I'M SORRY, BUT THIS IS GOING TO BE VERY PAINFUL!
NO!!
OH, JORDY, YOU LUNK-HEAD!

...YOU GODDAMN ·⟨SUCK⟩· STUPID LUNKHEAD! ·⟨SLURP⟩·

...FINGERS ARE ALL WEIRD AN' MOSSY AN'... AN'...

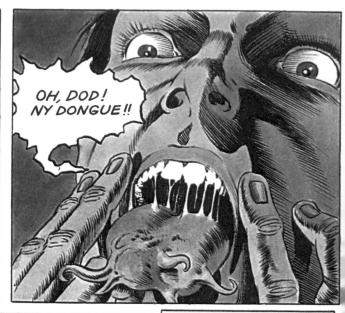

OH, DOD! NY DONGUE!!

MY... MY *TONGUE!* IT... IT'S *GROWIN'!* ...BECAUSE I WAS SUCKIN' MY *FINGERS!*

...NOT JUST YOUR TONGUE AND FINGERS, JORDY... YOU SHOULD SEE THE CRATER, HEH-HEH...

...AN' MY... MY *FACE!* WHERE I TOUCHED MY *CHEEK*...

NOT TO MENTION THE BUCKET ON THE PORCH...

EVERYTHING IS GROWING, JORDY! THE *CRATER*... THE *BUCKET*... AND *YOU!*

...*GROWIN'*... LORDY, *LORDY*... GROWIN'...

EVEN YOUR OWN FAVORITE *CHAIR*...

GROWIN'! RIGHT UNDER MY *HAND!!*

DOC GEESON! THIS TIME I GOT TO CALL HIM FOR SURE!

HELLO! THIS IS DOCTOR RICHARD GEESON...

DOC! DOC, THIS IS JORDY VERRILL-- OUT TO THE BLUE-BIRD CREEK? SOMETHING...

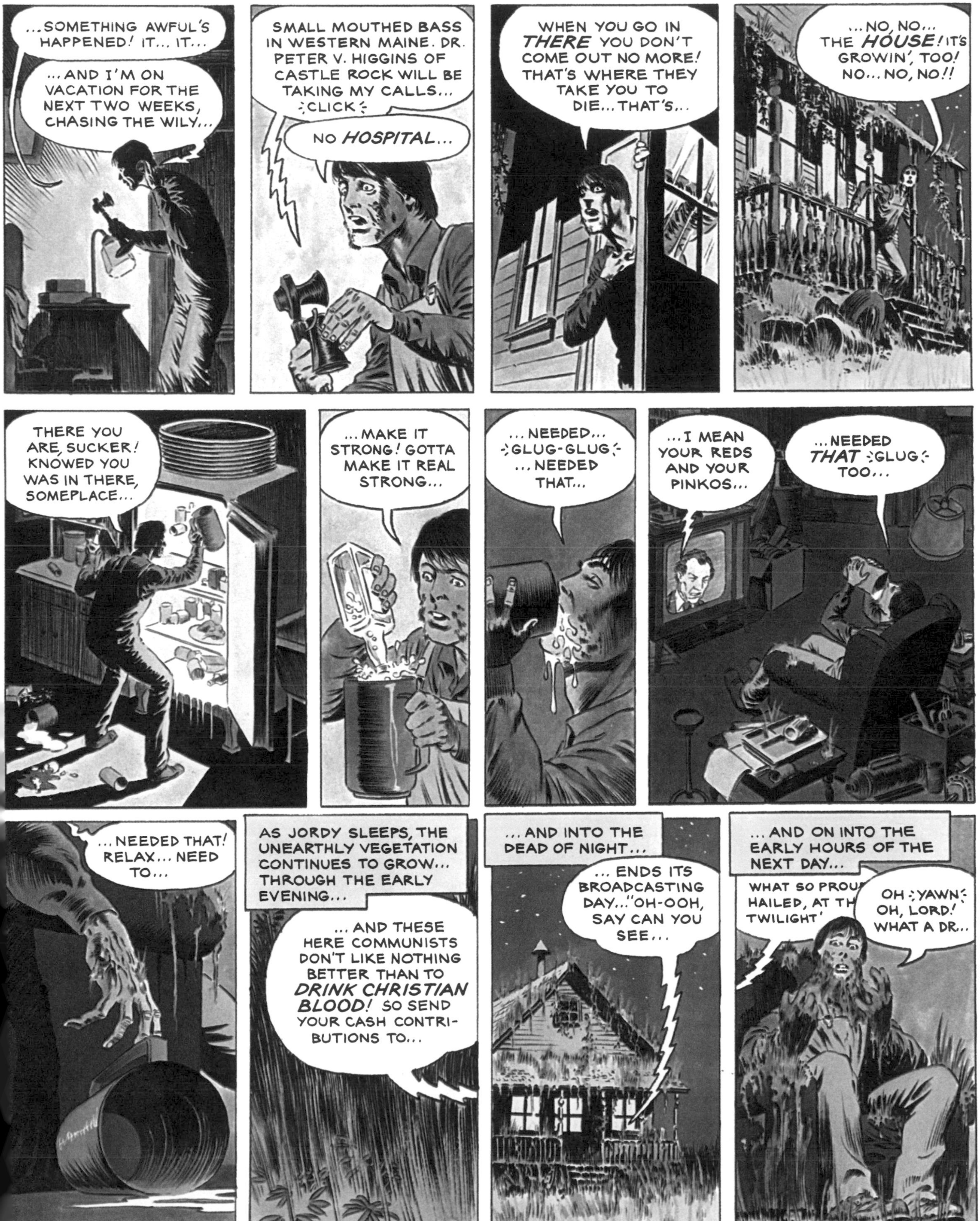
...SOMETHING AWFUL'S HAPPENED! IT... IT...
...AND I'M ON VACATION FOR THE NEXT TWO WEEKS, CHASING THE WILY...
SMALL MOUTHED BASS IN WESTERN MAINE. DR. PETER V. HIGGINS OF CASTLE ROCK WILL BE TAKING MY CALLS... CLICK
NO HOSPITAL...
WHEN YOU GO IN THERE YOU DON'T COME OUT NO MORE! THAT'S WHERE THEY TAKE YOU TO DIE... THAT'S...
...NO, NO... THE HOUSE! IT'S GROWIN', TOO! NO... NO, NO!!
THERE YOU ARE, SUCKER! KNOWED YOU WAS IN THERE, SOMEPLACE...
...MAKE IT STRONG! GOTTA MAKE IT REAL STRONG...
...NEEDED... GLUG-GLUG ...NEEDED THAT...
...I MEAN YOUR REDS AND YOUR PINKOS...
...NEEDED THAT GLUG TOO...
...NEEDED THAT! RELAX... NEED TO...
AS JORDY SLEEPS, THE UNEARTHLY VEGETATION CONTINUES TO GROW... THROUGH THE EARLY EVENING...
...AND THESE HERE COMMUNISTS DON'T LIKE NOTHING BETTER THAN TO DRINK CHRISTIAN BLOOD! SO SEND YOUR CASH CONTRI-BUTIONS TO...
...AND INTO THE DEAD OF NIGHT...
...ENDS ITS BROADCASTING DAY...'OH-OOH, SAY CAN YOU SEE...
...AND ON INTO THE EARLY HOURS OF THE NEXT DAY...
WHAT SO PROU HAILED, AT TH TWILIGHT'
OH YAWN OH, LORD! WHAT A DR...

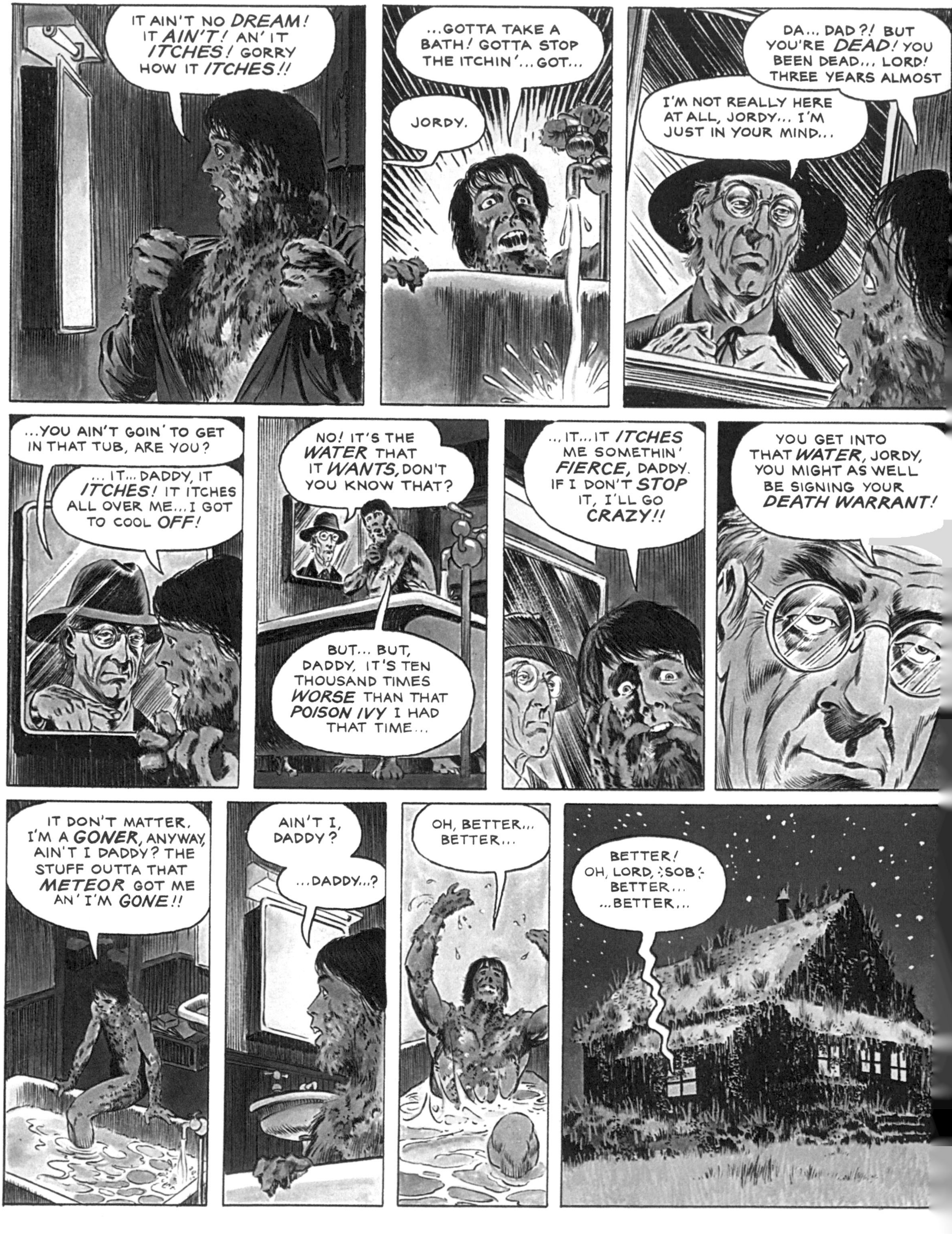
IT AIN'T NO DREAM! IT AIN'T! AN' IT ITCHES! GORRY HOW IT ITCHES!!
...GOTTA TAKE A BATH! GOTTA STOP THE ITCHIN'... GOT...
JORDY.
DA... DAD?! BUT YOU'RE DEAD! YOU BEEN DEAD... LORD! THREE YEARS ALMOST
I'M NOT REALLY HERE AT ALL, JORDY... I'M JUST IN YOUR MIND...
...YOU AIN'T GOIN' TO GET IN THAT TUB, ARE YOU?
... IT... DADDY, IT ITCHES! IT ITCHES ALL OVER ME... I GOT TO COOL OFF!
NO! IT'S THE WATER THAT IT WANTS, DON'T YOU KNOW THAT?
BUT... BUT, DADDY, IT'S TEN THOUSAND TIMES WORSE THAN THAT POISON IVY I HAD THAT TIME...
... IT... IT ITCHES ME SOMETHIN' FIERCE, DADDY. IF I DON'T STOP IT, I'LL GO CRAZY!!
YOU GET INTO THAT WATER, JORDY, YOU MIGHT AS WELL BE SIGNING YOUR DEATH WARRANT!
IT DON'T MATTER, I'M A GONER, ANYWAY, AIN'T I DADDY? THE STUFF OUTTA THAT METEOR GOT ME AN' I'M GONE!!
AIN'T I, DADDY?
...DADDY...?
OH, BETTER... BETTER...
BETTER! OH, LORD, -SOB- BETTER... ...BETTER...

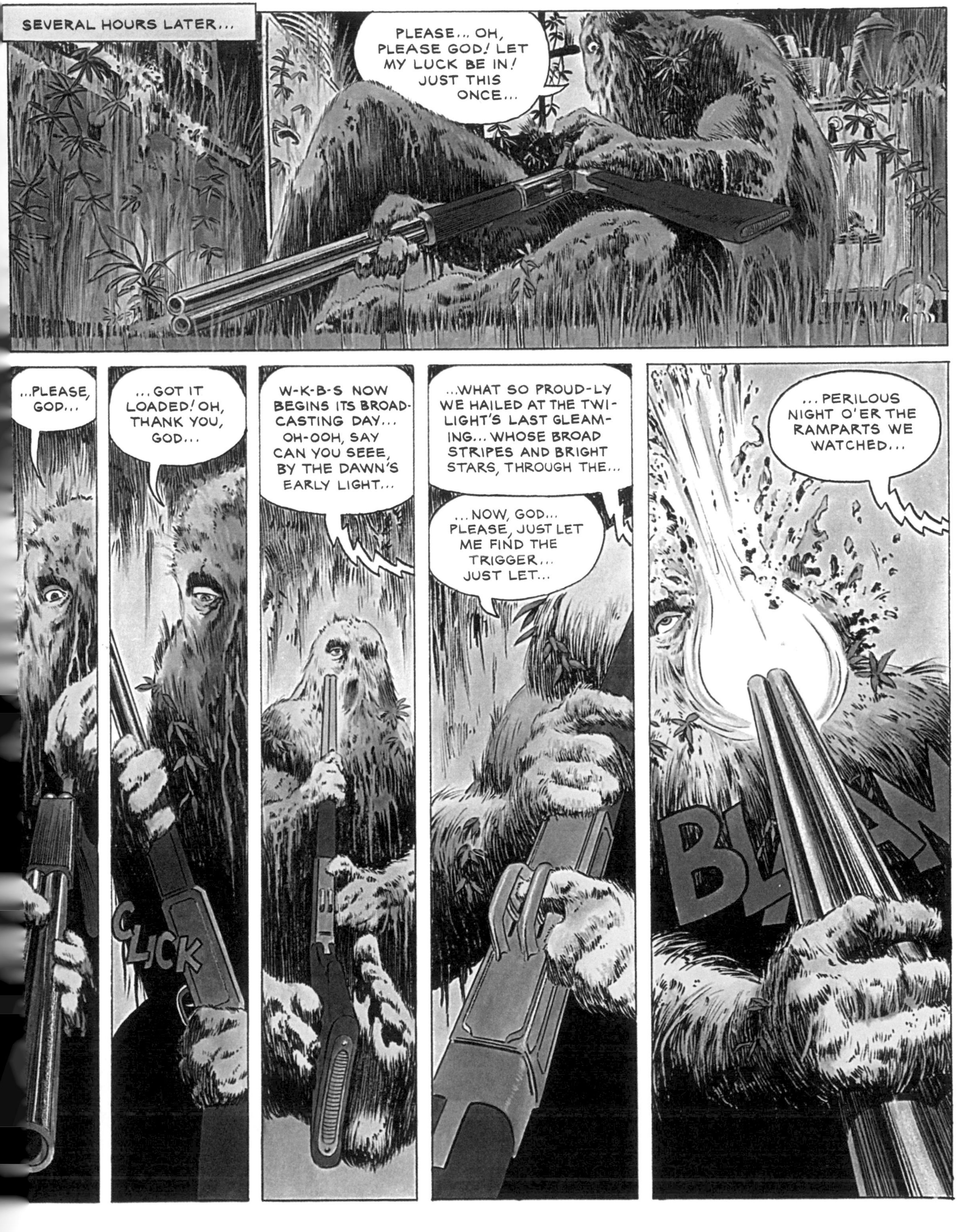
SEVERAL HOURS LATER...
PLEASE... OH, PLEASE GOD! LET MY LUCK BE IN! JUST THIS ONCE...
...PLEASE, GOD...
...GOT IT LOADED! OH, THANK YOU, GOD...
CLICK
W-K-B-S NOW BEGINS ITS BROAD-CASTING DAY... OH-OOH, SAY CAN YOU SEEE, BY THE DAWN'S EARLY LIGHT...
...WHAT SO PROUD-LY WE HAILED AT THE TWI-LIGHT'S LAST GLEAM-ING... WHOSE BROAD STRIPES AND BRIGHT STARS, THROUGH THE...
...NOW, GOD... PLEASE, JUST LET ME FIND THE TRIGGER... JUST LET...
...PERILOUS NIGHT O'ER THE RAMPARTS WE WATCHED...

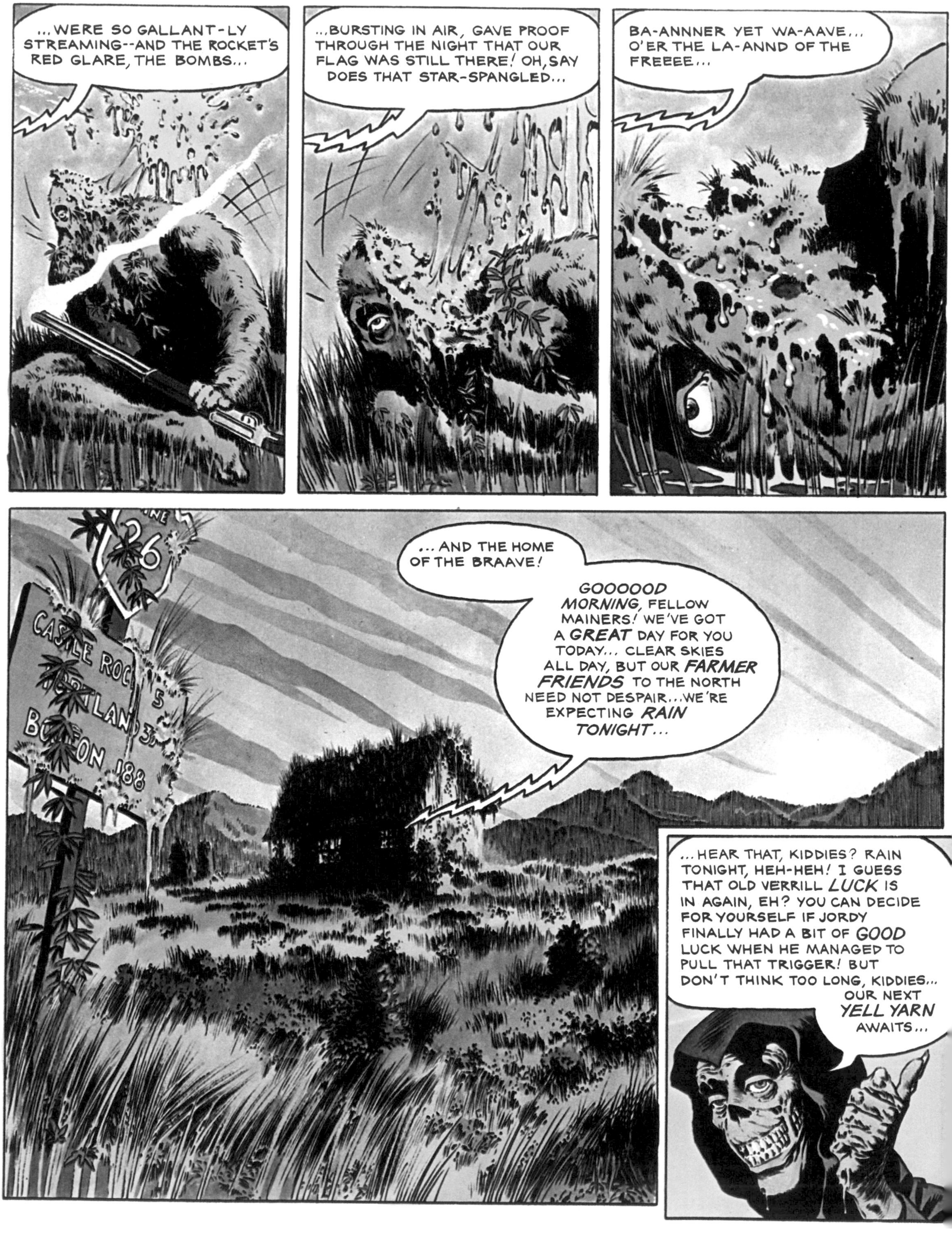
...WERE SO GALLANT-LY STREAMING--AND THE ROCKET'S RED GLARE, THE BOMBS...
...BURSTING IN AIR, GAVE PROOF THROUGH THE NIGHT THAT OUR FLAG WAS STILL THERE! OH, SAY DOES THAT STAR-SPANGLED...
BA-ANNNER YET WA-AAVE... O'ER THE LA-ANND OF THE FREEEE...
...AND THE HOME OF THE BRAAVE!
GOOOOOD MORNING, FELLOW MAINERS! WE'VE GOT A GREAT DAY FOR YOU TODAY... CLEAR SKIES ALL DAY, BUT OUR FARMER FRIENDS TO THE NORTH NEED NOT DESPAIR...WE'RE EXPECTING RAIN TONIGHT...
...HEAR THAT, KIDDIES? RAIN TONIGHT, HEH-HEH! I GUESS THAT OLD VERRILL LUCK IS IN AGAIN, EH? YOU CAN DECIDE FOR YOURSELF IF JORDY FINALLY HAD A BIT OF GOOD LUCK WHEN HE MANAGED TO PULL THAT TRIGGER! BUT DON'T THINK TOO LONG, KIDDIES... OUR NEXT YELL YARN AWAITS...

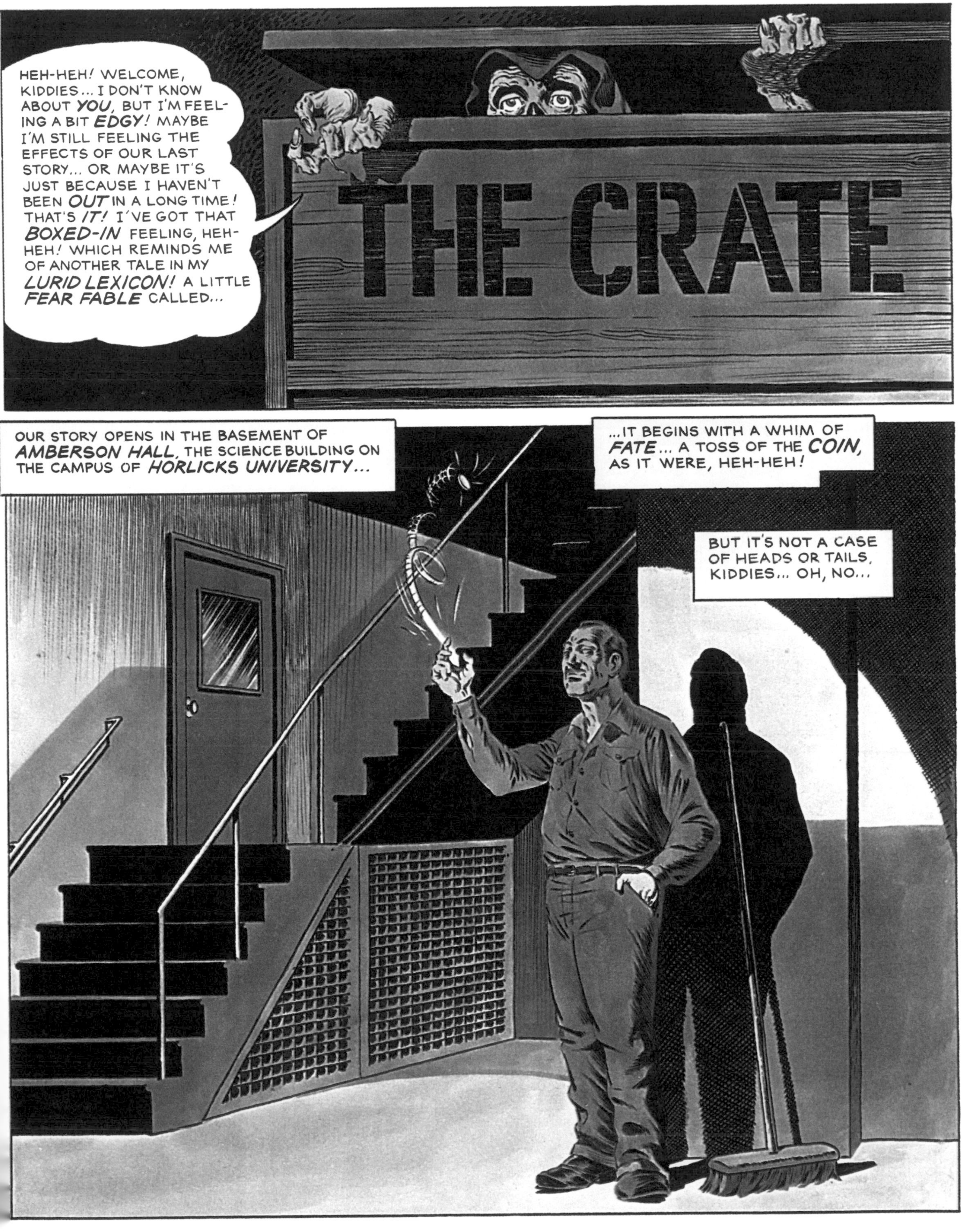
HEH-HEH! WELCOME, KIDDIES... I DON'T KNOW ABOUT YOU, BUT I'M FEELING A BIT EDGY! MAYBE I'M STILL FEELING THE EFFECTS OF OUR LAST STORY... OR MAYBE IT'S JUST BECAUSE I HAVEN'T BEEN OUT IN A LONG TIME! THAT'S IT! I'VE GOT THAT BOXED-IN FEELING, HEH-HEH! WHICH REMINDS ME OF ANOTHER TALE IN MY LURID LEXICON! A LITTLE FEAR FABLE CALLED...
THE CRATE
OUR STORY OPENS IN THE BASEMENT OF AMBERSON HALL, THE SCIENCE BUILDING ON THE CAMPUS OF HORLICKS UNIVERSITY...
...IT BEGINS WITH A WHIM OF FATE... A TOSS OF THE COIN, AS IT WERE, HEH-HEH!
BUT IT'S NOT A CASE OF HEADS OR TAILS, KIDDIES... OH, NO...

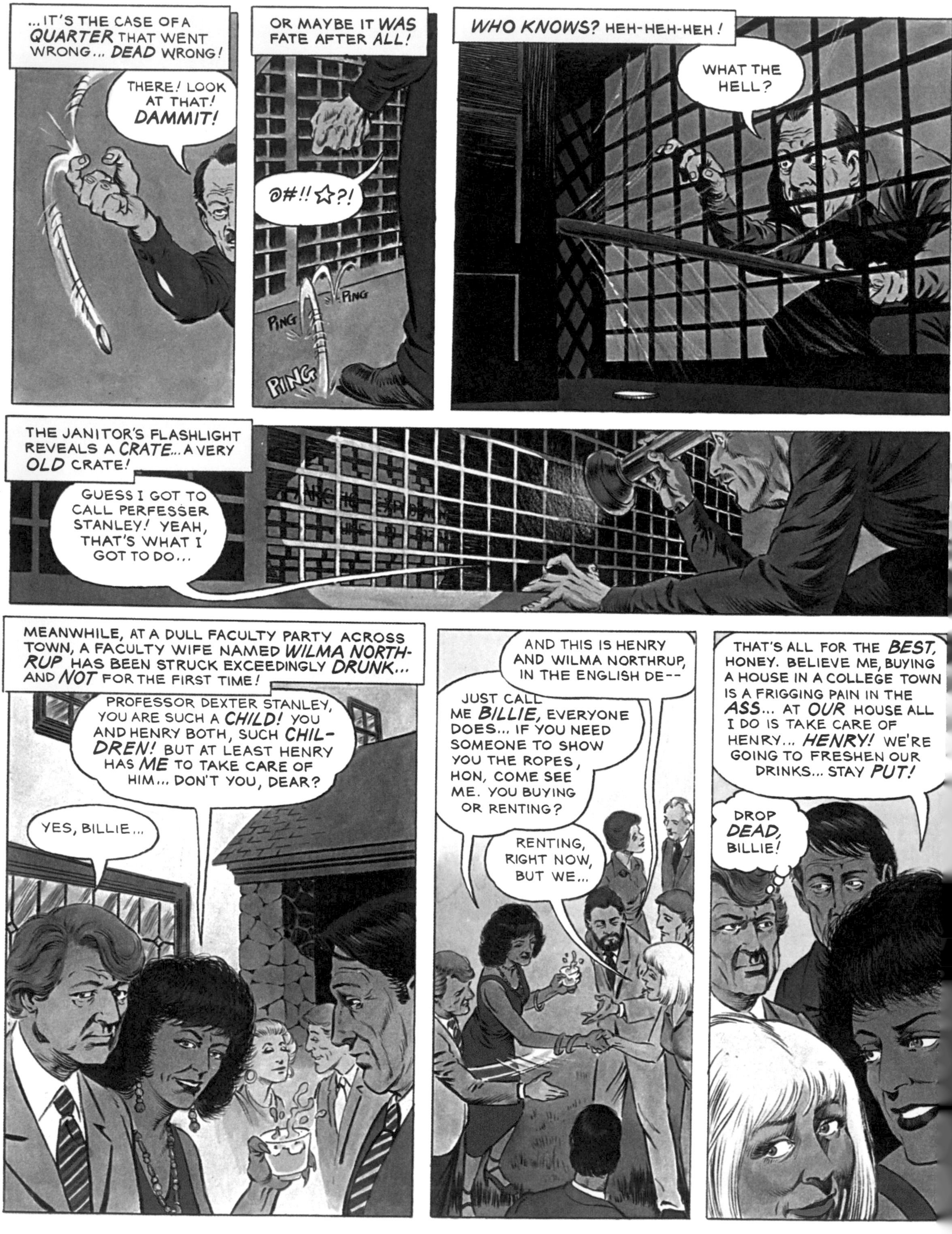
...IT'S THE CASE OF A QUARTER THAT WENT WRONG... DEAD WRONG!
THERE! LOOK AT THAT! DAMMIT!
OR MAYBE IT WAS FATE AFTER ALL!
@#!!☆?!
PING
PING
PING
WHO KNOWS? HEH-HEH-HEH!
WHAT THE HELL?
THE JANITOR'S FLASHLIGHT REVEALS A CRATE... A VERY OLD CRATE!
GUESS I GOT TO CALL PERFESSER STANLEY! YEAH, THAT'S WHAT I GOT TO DO...
MEANWHILE, AT A DULL FACULTY PARTY ACROSS TOWN, A FACULTY WIFE NAMED WILMA NORTHRUP HAS BEEN STRUCK EXCEEDINGLY DRUNK... AND NOT FOR THE FIRST TIME!
PROFESSOR DEXTER STANLEY, YOU ARE SUCH A CHILD! YOU AND HENRY BOTH, SUCH CHILDREN! BUT AT LEAST HENRY HAS ME TO TAKE CARE OF HIM... DON'T YOU, DEAR?
YES, BILLIE...
AND THIS IS HENRY AND WILMA NORTHRUP, IN THE ENGLISH DE--
JUST CALL ME BILLIE, EVERYONE DOES... IF YOU NEED SOMEONE TO SHOW YOU THE ROPES, HON, COME SEE ME. YOU BUYING OR RENTING?
RENTING, RIGHT NOW, BUT WE...
THAT'S ALL FOR THE BEST, HONEY. BELIEVE ME, BUYING A HOUSE IN A COLLEGE TOWN IS A FRIGGING PAIN IN THE ASS... AT OUR HOUSE ALL I DO IS TAKE CARE OF HENRY... HENRY! WE'RE GOING TO FRESHEN OUR DRINKS... STAY PUT!
DROP DEAD, BILLIE!

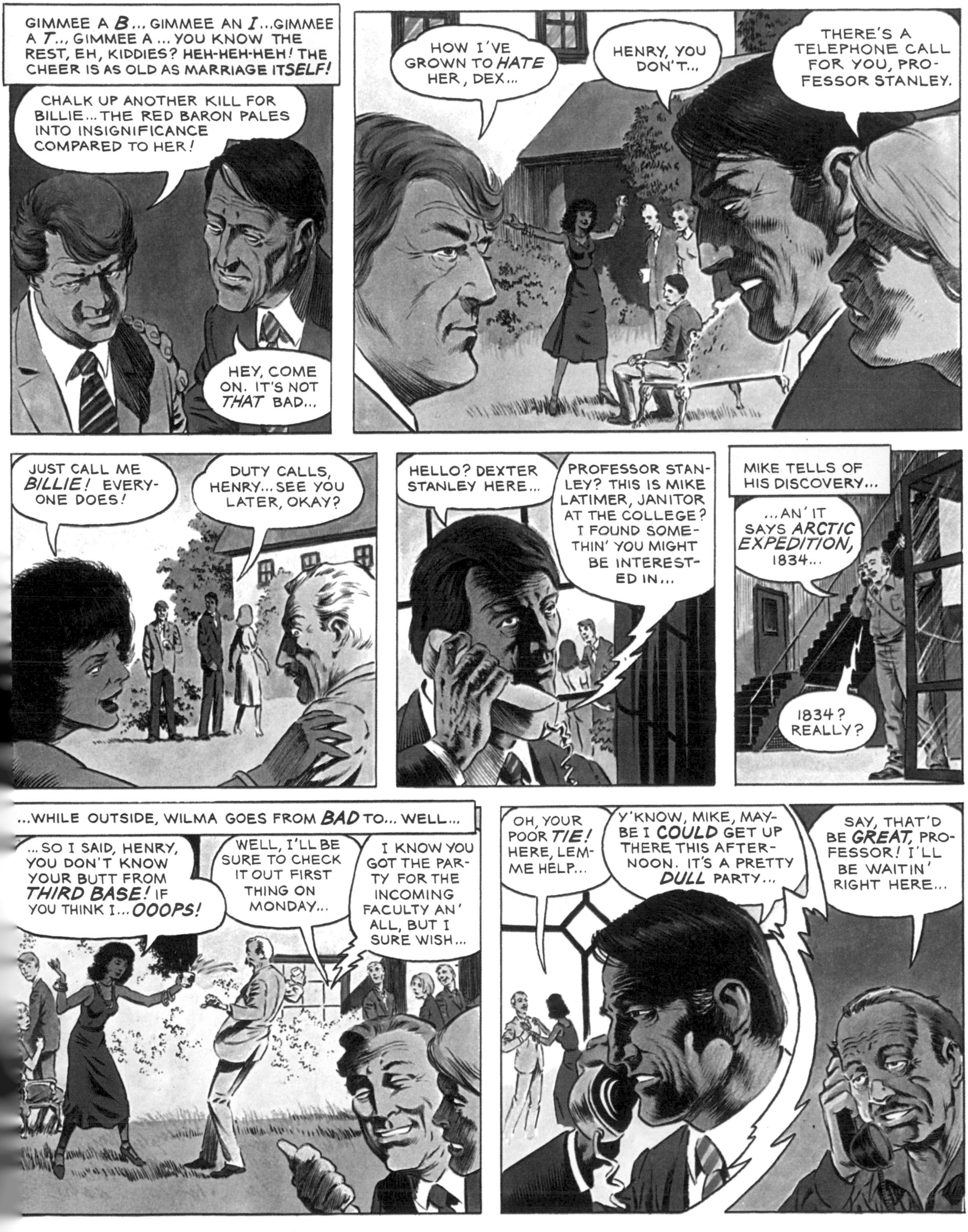
GIMMEE A B... GIMMEE AN I... GIMMEE A T..., GIMMEE A ... YOU KNOW THE REST, EH, KIDDIES? HEH-HEH-HEH! THE CHEER IS AS OLD AS MARRIAGE ITSELF!
CHALK UP ANOTHER KILL FOR BILLIE... THE RED BARON PALES INTO INSIGNIFICANCE COMPARED TO HER!
HEY, COME ON. IT'S NOT THAT BAD...
HOW I'VE GROWN TO HATE HER, DEX...
HENRY, YOU DON'T...
THERE'S A TELEPHONE CALL FOR YOU, PROFESSOR STANLEY.
JUST CALL ME BILLIE! EVERYONE DOES!
DUTY CALLS, HENRY... SEE YOU LATER, OKAY?
HELLO? DEXTER STANLEY HERE...
PROFESSOR STANLEY? THIS IS MIKE LATIMER, JANITOR AT THE COLLEGE? I FOUND SOMETHIN' YOU MIGHT BE INTERESTED IN...
MIKE TELLS OF HIS DISCOVERY...
...AN' IT SAYS ARCTIC EXPEDITION, 1834...
1834? REALLY?
...WHILE OUTSIDE, WILMA GOES FROM BAD TO... WELL...
...SO I SAID, HENRY, YOU DON'T KNOW YOUR BUTT FROM THIRD BASE! IF YOU THINK I... OOOPS!
WELL, I'LL BE SURE TO CHECK IT OUT FIRST THING ON MONDAY...
I KNOW YOU GOT THE PARTY FOR THE INCOMING FACULTY AN' ALL, BUT I SURE WISH...
OH, YOUR POOR TIE! HERE, LEMME HELP...
Y'KNOW, MIKE, MAYBE I COULD GET UP THERE THIS AFTERNOON. IT'S A PRETTY DULL PARTY...
SAY, THAT'D BE GREAT, PROFESSOR! I'LL BE WAITIN' RIGHT HERE...

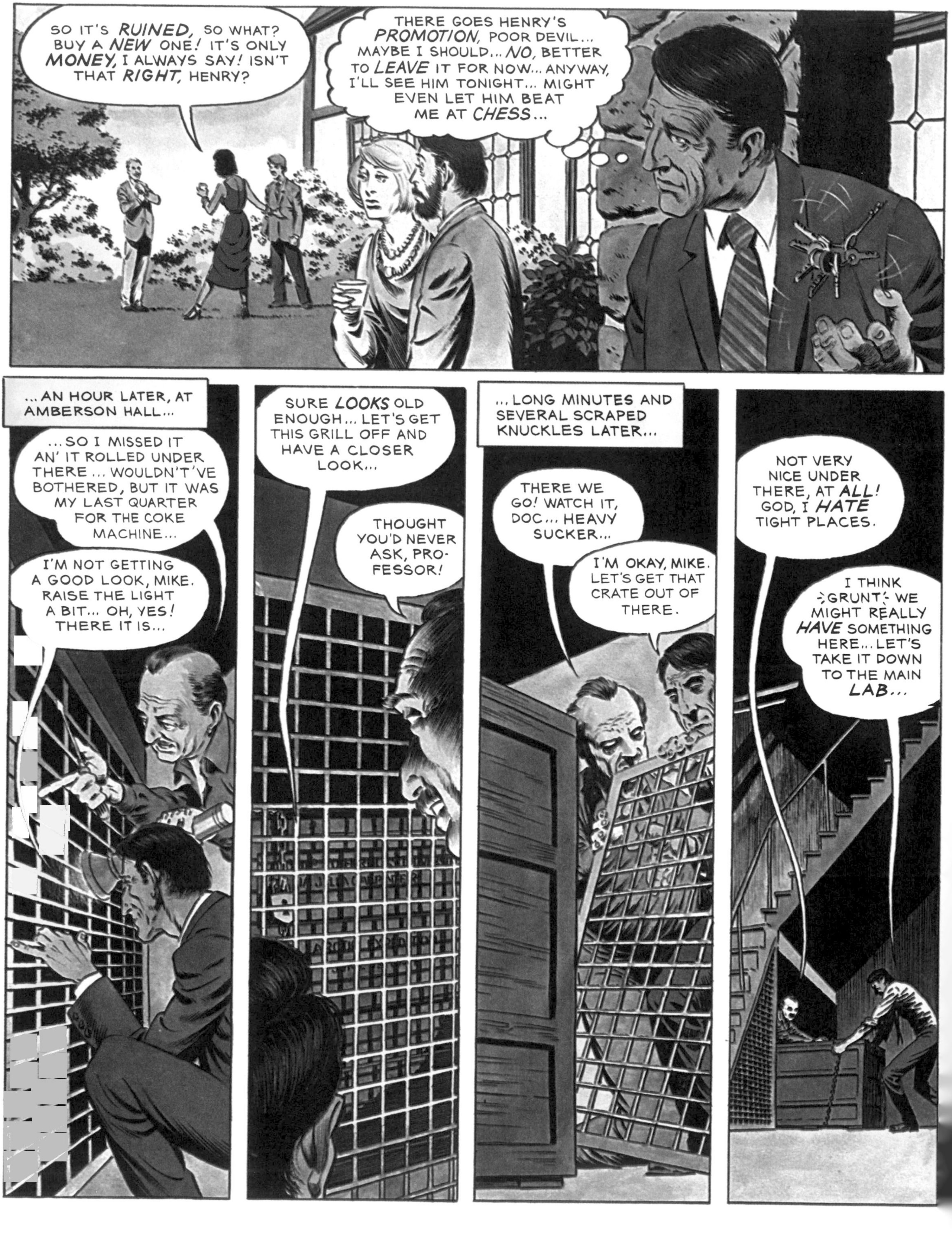
SO IT'S RUINED, SO WHAT? BUY A NEW ONE! IT'S ONLY MONEY, I ALWAYS SAY! ISN'T THAT RIGHT, HENRY?
THERE GOES HENRY'S PROMOTION, POOR DEVIL... MAYBE I SHOULD... NO, BETTER TO LEAVE IT FOR NOW... ANYWAY, I'LL SEE HIM TONIGHT... MIGHT EVEN LET HIM BEAT ME AT CHESS...
...AN HOUR LATER, AT AMBERSON HALL...
...SO I MISSED IT AN' IT ROLLED UNDER THERE ... WOULDN'T'VE BOTHERED, BUT IT WAS MY LAST QUARTER FOR THE COKE MACHINE...
I'M NOT GETTING A GOOD LOOK, MIKE. RAISE THE LIGHT A BIT... OH, YES! THERE IT IS...
SURE LOOKS OLD ENOUGH... LET'S GET THIS GRILL OFF AND HAVE A CLOSER LOOK...
THOUGHT YOU'D NEVER ASK, PRO-FESSOR!
...LONG MINUTES AND SEVERAL SCRAPED KNUCKLES LATER...
THERE WE GO! WATCH IT, DOC... HEAVY SUCKER...
I'M OKAY, MIKE. LET'S GET THAT CRATE OUT OF THERE.
NOT VERY NICE UNDER THERE, AT ALL! GOD, I HATE TIGHT PLACES.
I THINK -GRUNT- WE MIGHT REALLY HAVE SOMETHING HERE... LET'S TAKE IT DOWN TO THE MAIN LAB...

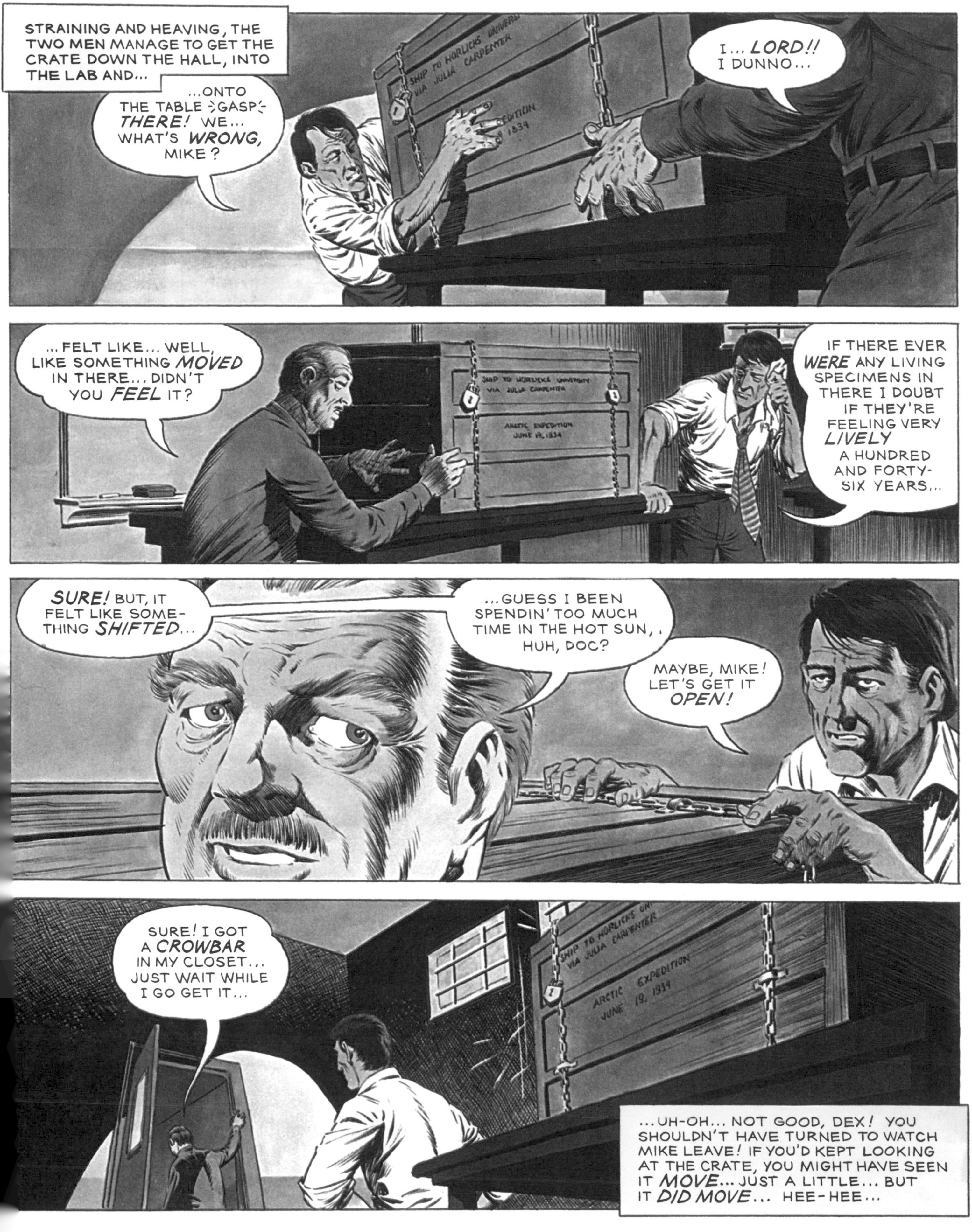
STRAINING AND HEAVING, THE TWO MEN MANAGE TO GET THE CRATE DOWN THE HALL, INTO THE LAB AND...
...ONTO THE TABLE -GASP- THERE! WE... WHAT'S WRONG, MIKE?
I... LORD!! I DUNNO...
SHIP TO HORLICKS UNIVERSITY VIA JULIA CARPENTER
...FELT LIKE... WELL, LIKE SOMETHING MOVED IN THERE... DIDN'T YOU FEEL IT?
IF THERE EVER WERE ANY LIVING SPECIMENS IN THERE I DOUBT IF THEY'RE FEELING VERY LIVELY A HUNDRED AND FORTY-SIX YEARS...
ARCTIC EXPEDITION JUNE 19, 1834
SURE! BUT, IT FELT LIKE SOMETHING SHIFTED...
...GUESS I BEEN SPENDIN' TOO MUCH TIME IN THE HOT SUN,. HUH, DOC?
MAYBE, MIKE! LET'S GET IT OPEN!
SURE! I GOT A CROWBAR IN MY CLOSET... JUST WAIT WHILE I GO GET IT...
...UH-OH... NOT GOOD, DEX! YOU SHOULDN'T HAVE TURNED TO WATCH MIKE LEAVE! IF YOU'D KEPT LOOKING AT THE CRATE, YOU MIGHT HAVE SEEN IT MOVE... JUST A LITTLE... BUT IT DID MOVE... HEE-HEE...

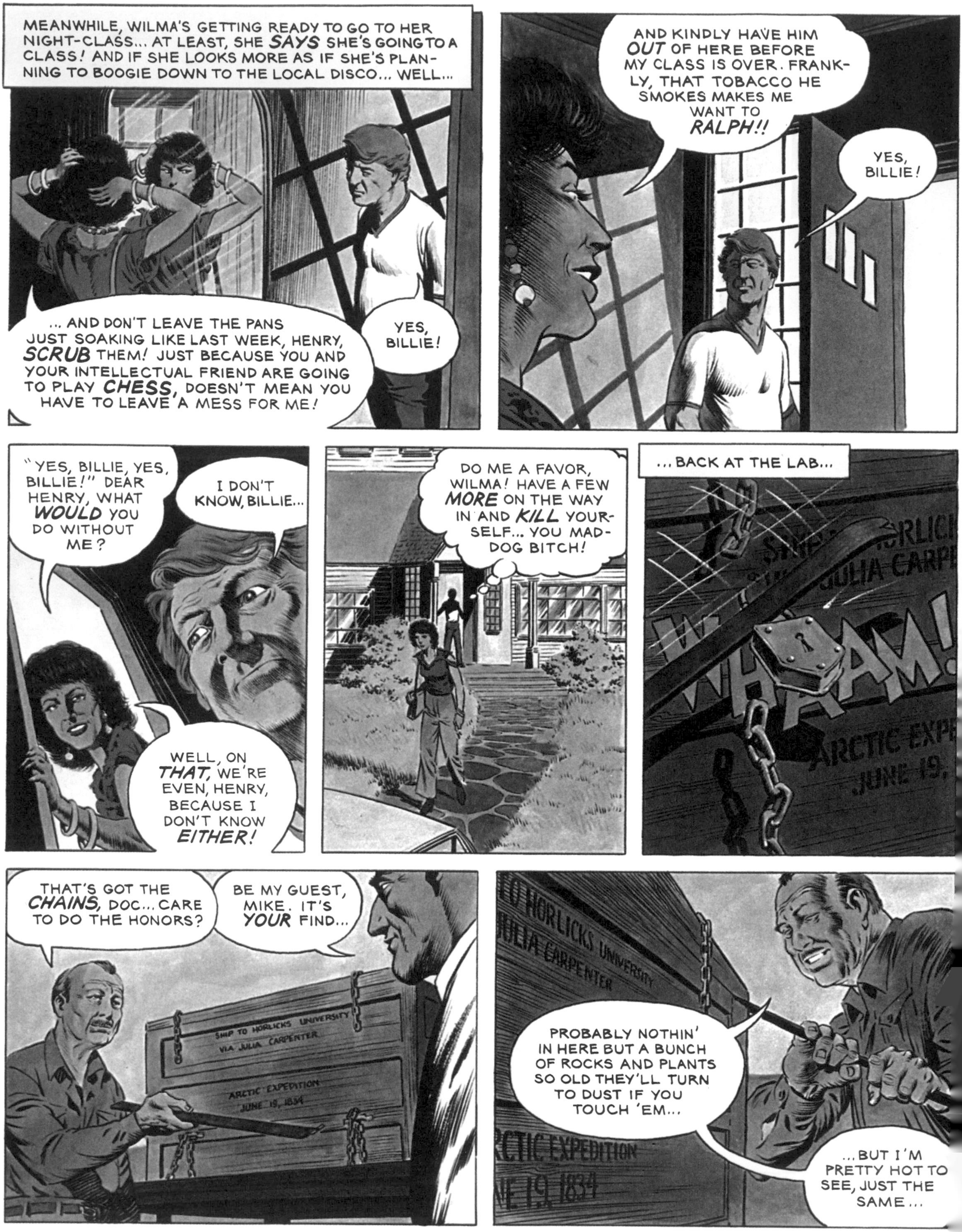
MEANWHILE, WILMA'S GETTING READY TO GO TO HER NIGHT-CLASS... AT LEAST, SHE SAYS SHE'S GOING TO A CLASS! AND IF SHE LOOKS MORE AS IF SHE'S PLANNING TO BOOGIE DOWN TO THE LOCAL DISCO... WELL...
... AND DON'T LEAVE THE PANS JUST SOAKING LIKE LAST WEEK, HENRY, SCRUB THEM! JUST BECAUSE YOU AND YOUR INTELLECTUAL FRIEND ARE GOING TO PLAY CHESS, DOESN'T MEAN YOU HAVE TO LEAVE A MESS FOR ME!
YES, BILLIE!
AND KINDLY HAVE HIM OUT OF HERE BEFORE MY CLASS IS OVER. FRANKLY, THAT TOBACCO HE SMOKES MAKES ME WANT TO RALPH!!
YES, BILLIE!
"YES, BILLIE, YES, BILLIE!" DEAR HENRY, WHAT WOULD YOU DO WITHOUT ME?
I DON'T KNOW, BILLIE...
WELL, ON THAT, WE'RE EVEN, HENRY, BECAUSE I DON'T KNOW EITHER!
DO ME A FAVOR, WILMA! HAVE A FEW MORE ON THE WAY IN AND KILL YOURSELF... YOU MAD-DOG BITCH!
... BACK AT THE LAB...
WHAAM!
THAT'S GOT THE CHAINS, DOC... CARE TO DO THE HONORS?
BE MY GUEST, MIKE. IT'S YOUR FIND...
SHIP TO HORLICKS UNIVERSITY
VIA JULIA CARPENTER
ARCTIC EXPEDITION
JUNE 19, 1834
PROBABLY NOTHIN' IN HERE BUT A BUNCH OF ROCKS AND PLANTS SO OLD THEY'LL TURN TO DUST IF YOU TOUCH 'EM...
... BUT I'M PRETTY HOT TO SEE, JUST THE SAME...

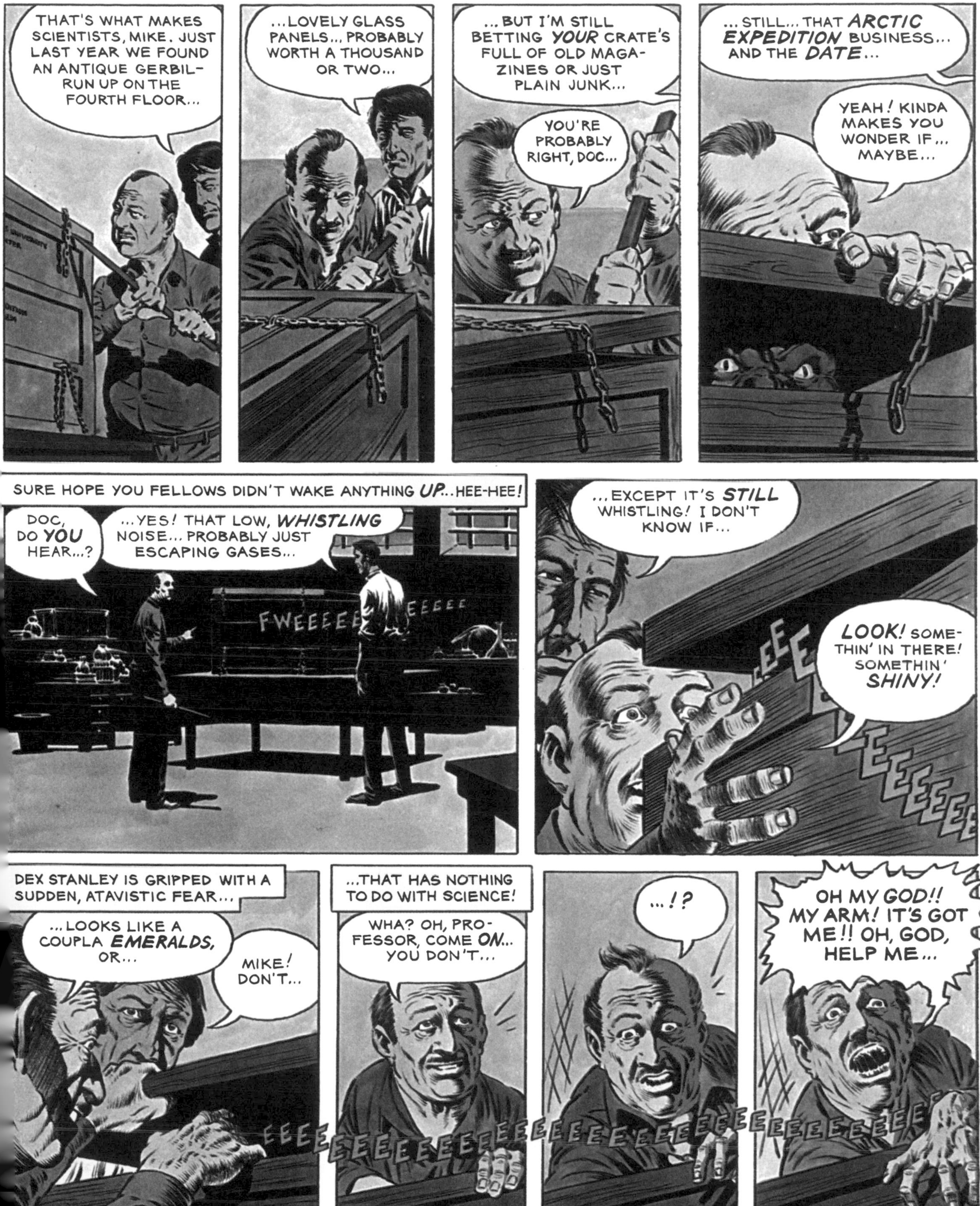
THAT'S WHAT MAKES SCIENTISTS, MIKE. JUST LAST YEAR WE FOUND AN ANTIQUE GERBIL-RUN UP ON THE FOURTH FLOOR...
...LOVELY GLASS PANELS... PROBABLY WORTH A THOUSAND OR TWO...
...BUT I'M STILL BETTING YOUR CRATE'S FULL OF OLD MAGA-ZINES OR JUST PLAIN JUNK...
YOU'RE PROBABLY RIGHT, DOC...
...STILL... THAT ARCTIC EXPEDITION BUSINESS... AND THE DATE...
YEAH! KINDA MAKES YOU WONDER IF... MAYBE...
SURE HOPE YOU FELLOWS DIDN'T WAKE ANYTHING UP.. HEE-HEE!
DOC, DO YOU HEAR...?
...YES! THAT LOW, WHISTLING NOISE... PROBABLY JUST ESCAPING GASES...
FWEEEEEEEEEEE
...EXCEPT IT'S STILL WHISTLING! I DON'T KNOW IF...
LOOK! SOME-THIN' IN THERE! SOMETHIN' SHINY!
EEEEEEEE
DEX STANLEY IS GRIPPED WITH A SUDDEN, ATAVISTIC FEAR...
...LOOKS LIKE A COUPLA EMERALDS, OR...
MIKE! DON'T...
...THAT HAS NOTHING TO DO WITH SCIENCE!
WHA? OH, PRO-FESSOR, COME ON... YOU DON'T...
...!?
OH MY GOD!! MY ARM! IT'S GOT ME!! OH, GOD, HELP ME...
EEEEEEEEEEEEEEEEEEEEEEEEEEEEEE

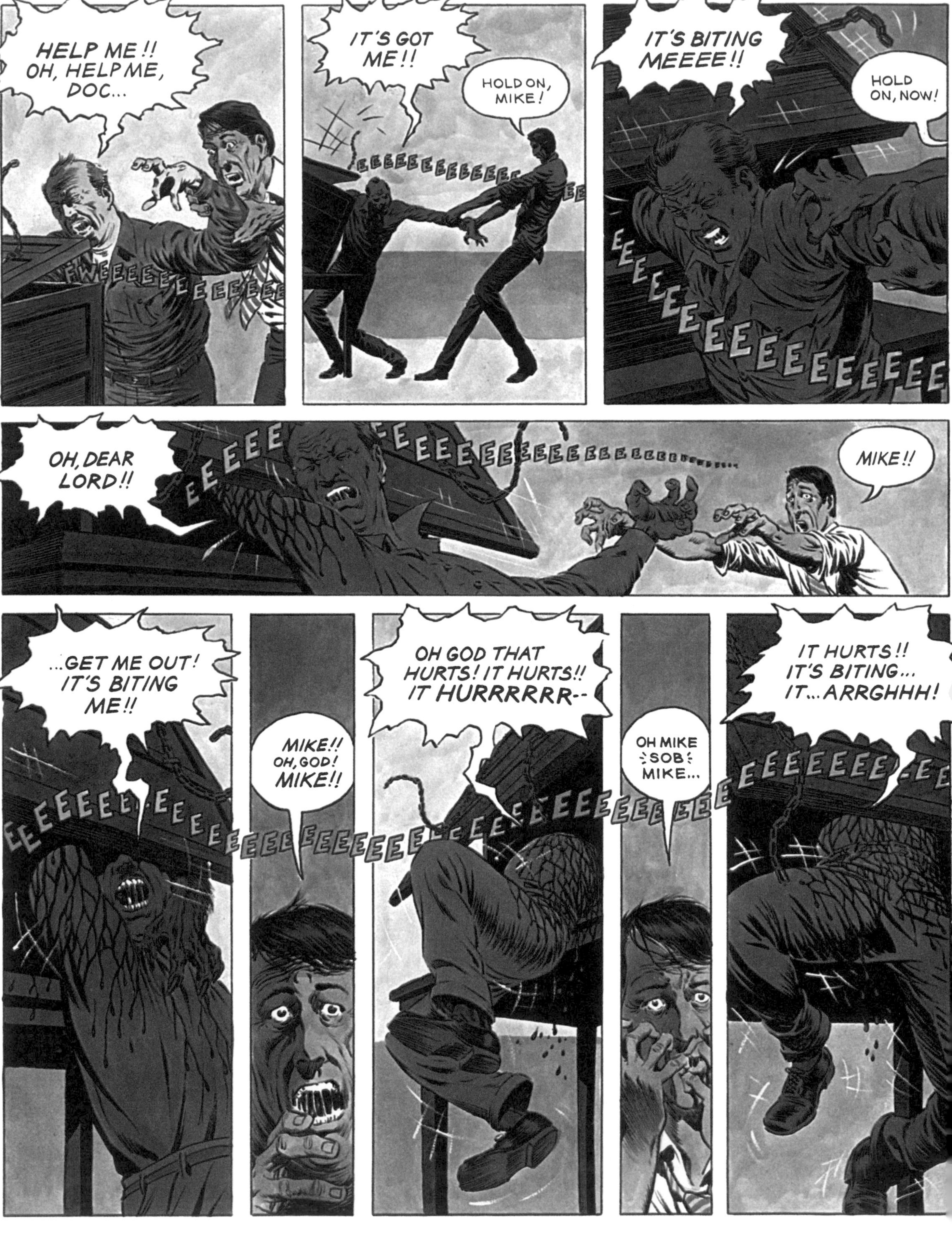
HELP ME!! OH, HELP ME, DOC...
IT'S GOT ME!!
HOLD ON, MIKE!
IT'S BITING MEEEE!!
HOLD ON, NOW!
OH, DEAR LORD!!
MIKE!!
...GET ME OUT! IT'S BITING ME!!
MIKE!! OH, GOD! MIKE!!
OH GOD THAT HURTS! IT HURTS!! IT HURRRRRR--
OH MIKE :SOB: MIKE...
IT HURTS!! IT'S BITING... IT... ARRGHHH!

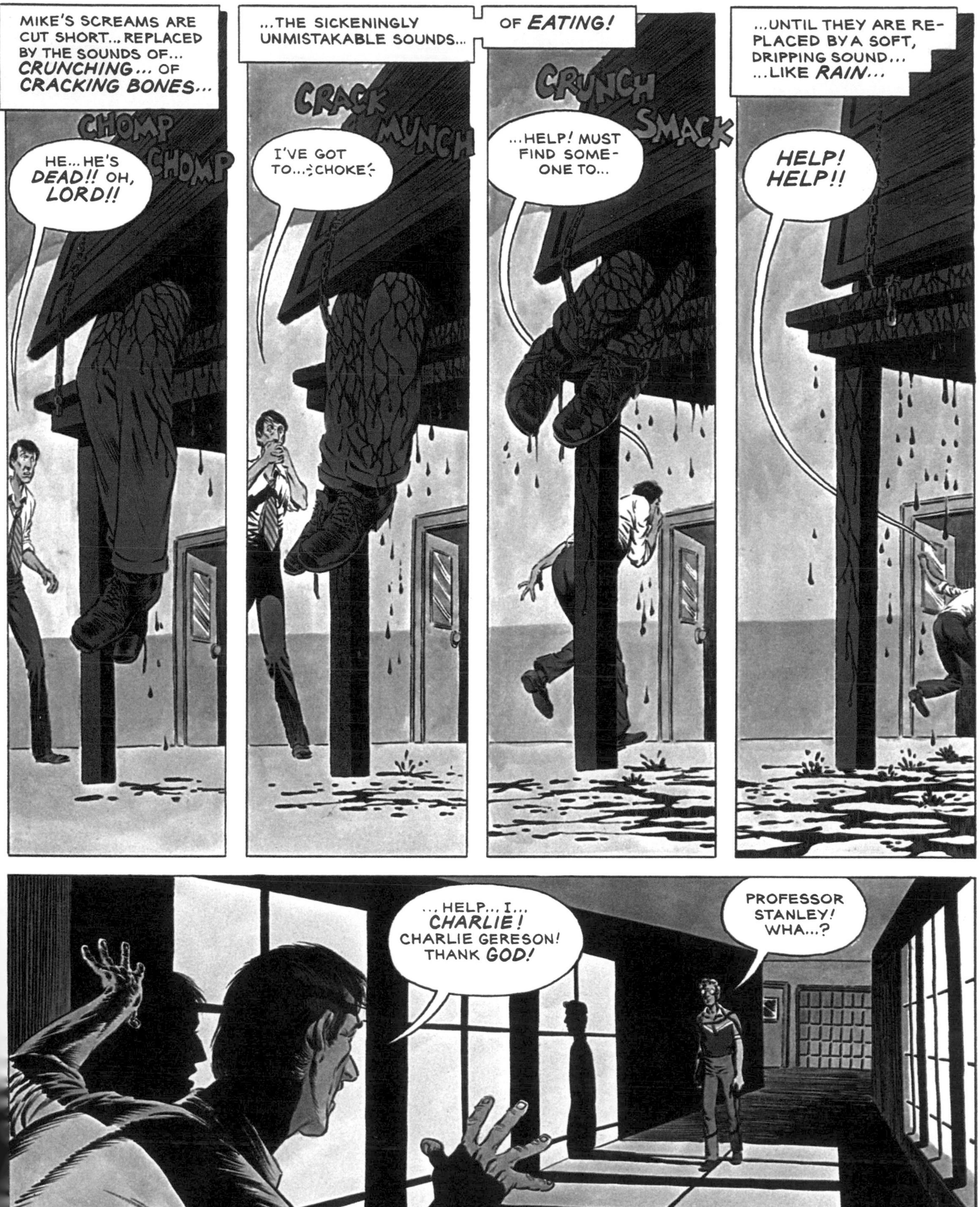

MIKE'S SCREAMS ARE CUT SHORT... REPLACED BY THE SOUNDS OF... CRUNCHING... OF CRACKING BONES...
CHOMP CHOMP
HE... HE'S DEAD!! OH, LORD!!
...THE SICKENINGLY UNMISTAKABLE SOUNDS...
CRACK MUNCH
I'VE GOT TO... CHOKE
OF EATING!
CRUNCH SMACK
...HELP! MUST FIND SOME-ONE TO...
...UNTIL THEY ARE RE-PLACED BY A SOFT, DRIPPING SOUND... ...LIKE RAIN...
HELP! HELP!!
..., HELP... I... CHARLIE! CHARLIE GERESON! THANK GOD!
PROFESSOR STANLEY! WHA...?

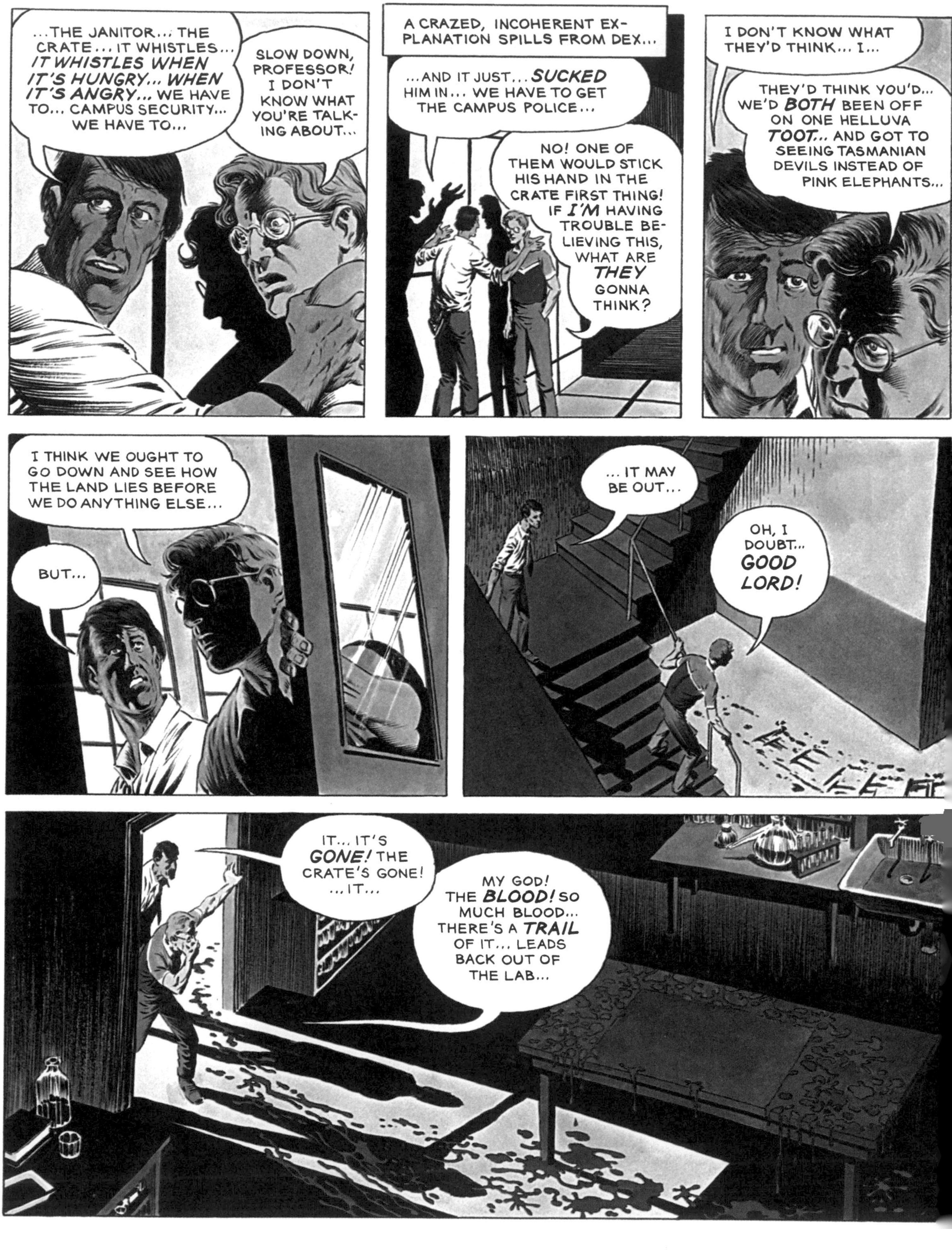

...THE JANITOR... THE CRATE... IT WHISTLES... IT WHISTLES WHEN IT'S HUNGRY... WHEN IT'S ANGRY... WE HAVE TO... CAMPUS SECURITY... WE HAVE TO...
SLOW DOWN, PROFESSOR! I DON'T KNOW WHAT YOU'RE TALKING ABOUT...
A CRAZED, INCOHERENT EXPLANATION SPILLS FROM DEX...
...AND IT JUST... SUCKED HIM IN... WE HAVE TO GET THE CAMPUS POLICE...
NO! ONE OF THEM WOULD STICK HIS HAND IN THE CRATE FIRST THING! IF I'M HAVING TROUBLE BELIEVING THIS, WHAT ARE THEY GONNA THINK?
I DON'T KNOW WHAT THEY'D THINK... I...
THEY'D THINK YOU'D... WE'D BOTH BEEN OFF ON ONE HELLUVA TOOT... AND GOT TO SEEING TASMANIAN DEVILS INSTEAD OF PINK ELEPHANTS...
I THINK WE OUGHT TO GO DOWN AND SEE HOW THE LAND LIES BEFORE WE DO ANYTHING ELSE...
BUT...
... IT MAY BE OUT...
OH, I DOUBT... GOOD LORD!
IT... IT'S GONE! THE CRATE'S GONE! ...IT...
MY GOD! THE BLOOD! SO MUCH BLOOD... THERE'S A TRAIL OF IT... LEADS BACK OUT OF THE LAB...

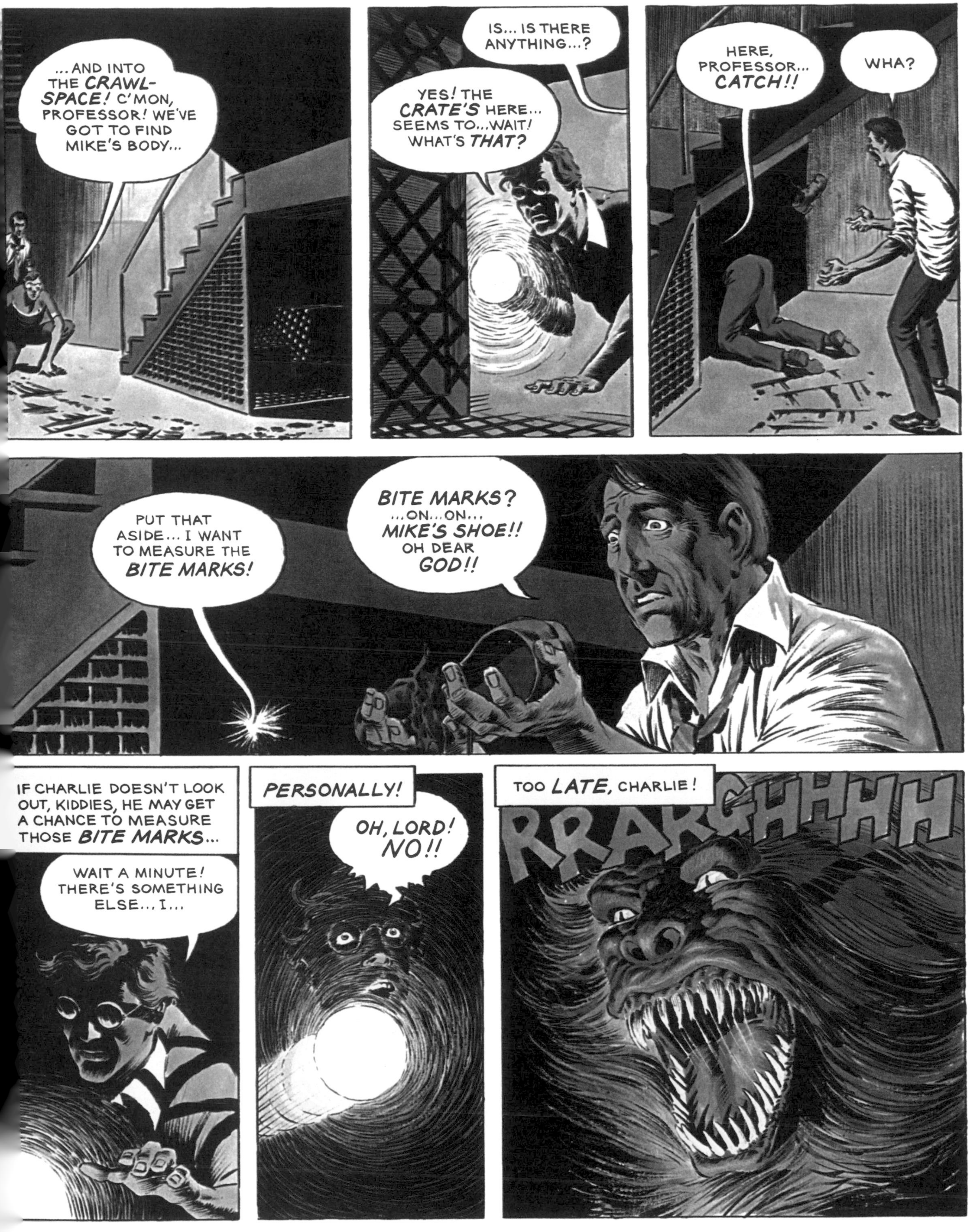
...AND INTO THE CRAWL-SPACE! C'MON, PROFESSOR! WE'VE GOT TO FIND MIKE'S BODY...
IS... IS THERE ANYTHING...?
YES! THE CRATE'S HERE... SEEMS TO...WAIT! WHAT'S THAT?
HERE, PROFESSOR... CATCH!!
WHA?
PUT THAT ASIDE... I WANT TO MEASURE THE BITE MARKS!
BITE MARKS? ...ON...ON... MIKE'S SHOE!! OH DEAR GOD!!
IF CHARLIE DOESN'T LOOK OUT, KIDDIES, HE MAY GET A CHANCE TO MEASURE THOSE BITE MARKS...
WAIT A MINUTE! THERE'S SOMETHING ELSE..., I...
PERSONALLY!
OH, LORD! NO!!
TOO LATE, CHARLIE!
RRARGHHHH

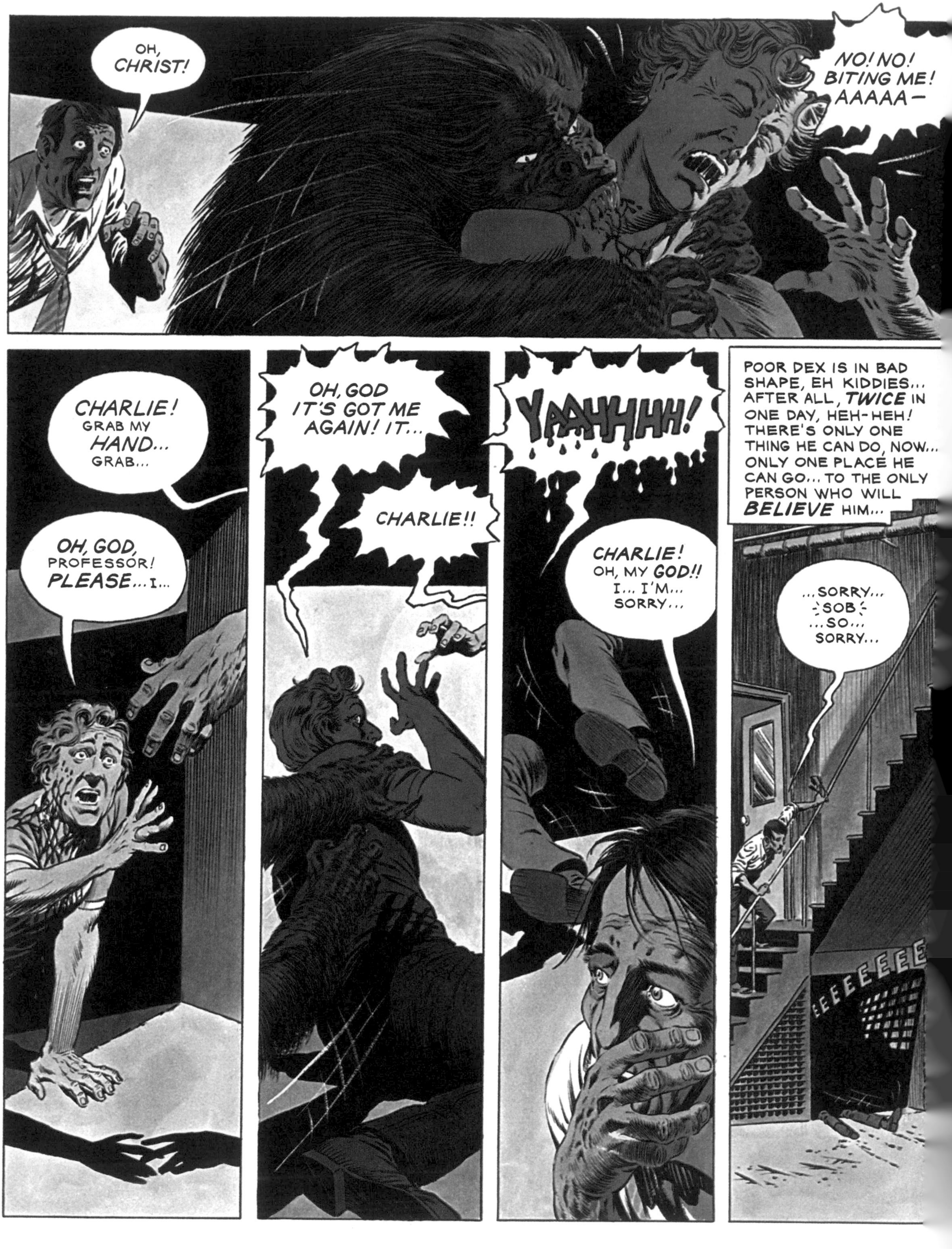
OH, CHRIST!
NO! NO! BITING ME! AAAAA—
CHARLIE! GRAB MY HAND... GRAB...
OH, GOD, PROFESSOR! PLEASE... I...
OH, GOD IT'S GOT ME AGAIN! IT...
CHARLIE!!
YAAHHHH!
CHARLIE! OH, MY GOD!! I... I'M... SORRY...
POOR DEX IS IN BAD SHAPE, EH KIDDIES... AFTER ALL, TWICE IN ONE DAY, HEH-HEH! THERE'S ONLY ONE THING HE CAN DO, NOW... ONLY ONE PLACE HE CAN GO... TO THE ONLY PERSON WHO WILL BELIEVE HIM...
...SORRY... SOB ...SO... SORRY...
EEEEEEE

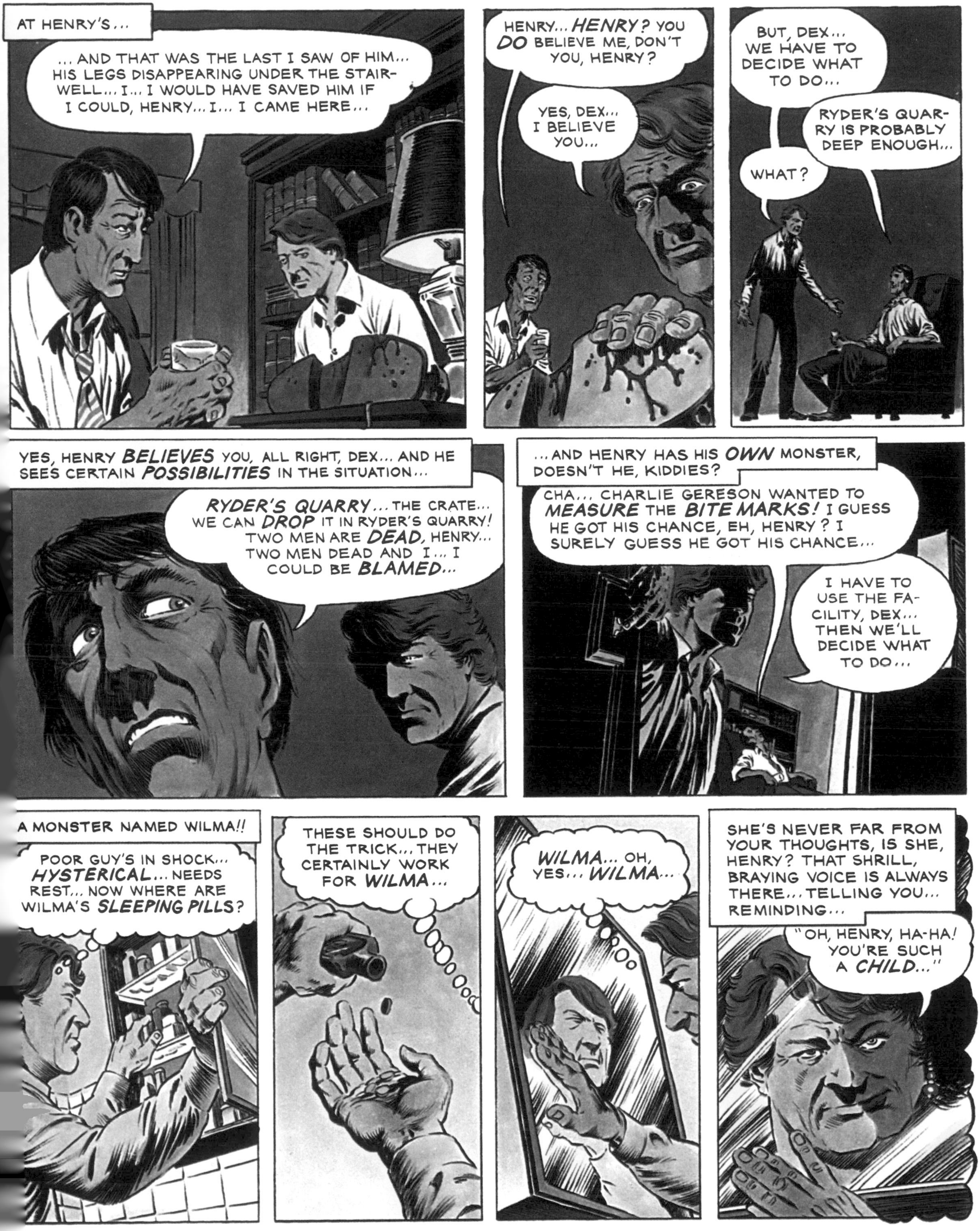
AT HENRY'S...
...AND THAT WAS THE LAST I SAW OF HIM... HIS LEGS DISAPPEARING UNDER THE STAIRWELL... I... I WOULD HAVE SAVED HIM IF I COULD, HENRY... I... I CAME HERE...
HENRY... HENRY? YOU DO BELIEVE ME, DON'T YOU, HENRY?
YES, DEX... I BELIEVE YOU...
BUT, DEX... WE HAVE TO DECIDE WHAT TO DO...
WHAT?
RYDER'S QUARRY IS PROBABLY DEEP ENOUGH...
YES, HENRY BELIEVES YOU, ALL RIGHT, DEX... AND HE SEES CERTAIN POSSIBILITIES IN THE SITUATION...
RYDER'S QUARRY... THE CRATE... WE CAN DROP IT IN RYDER'S QUARRY! TWO MEN ARE DEAD, HENRY... TWO MEN DEAD AND I... I COULD BE BLAMED...
...AND HENRY HAS HIS OWN MONSTER, DOESN'T HE, KIDDIES?
CHA... CHARLIE GERESON WANTED TO MEASURE THE BITE MARKS! I GUESS HE GOT HIS CHANCE, EH, HENRY? I SURELY GUESS HE GOT HIS CHANCE...
I HAVE TO USE THE FACILITY, DEX... THEN WE'LL DECIDE WHAT TO DO...
A MONSTER NAMED WILMA!!
POOR GUY'S IN SHOCK... HYSTERICAL... NEEDS REST... NOW WHERE ARE WILMA'S SLEEPING PILLS?
THESE SHOULD DO THE TRICK... THEY CERTAINLY WORK FOR WILMA...
WILMA... OH, YES... WILMA...
SHE'S NEVER FAR FROM YOUR THOUGHTS, IS SHE, HENRY? THAT SHRILL, BRAYING VOICE IS ALWAYS THERE... TELLING YOU... REMINDING...
"OH, HENRY, HA-HA! YOU'RE SUCH A CHILD..."

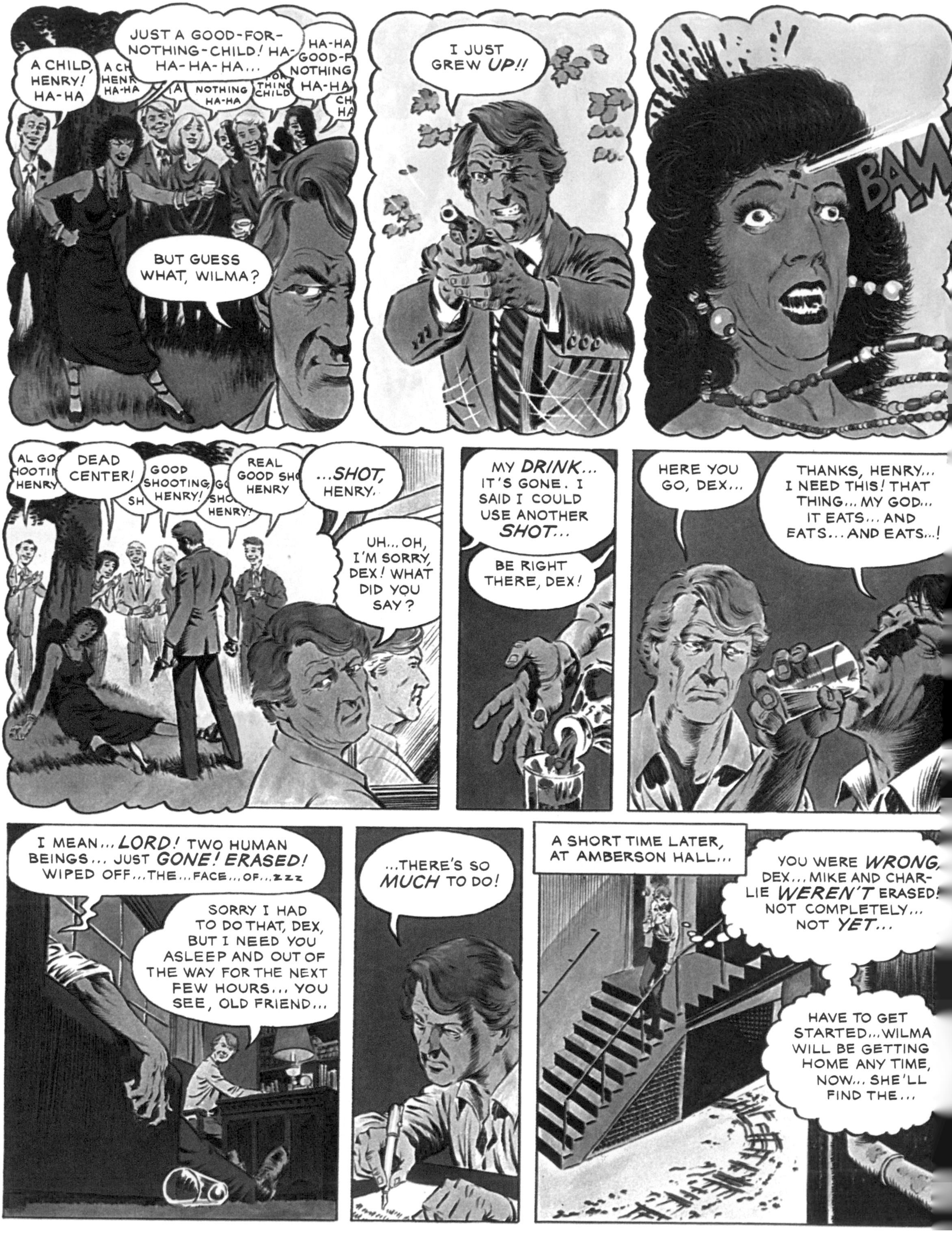
A CHILD, HENRY! HA-HA
JUST A GOOD-FOR-NOTHING-CHILD! HA-HA-HA-HA...
NOTHING HA-HA
BUT GUESS WHAT, WILMA?
I JUST GREW UP!!
DEAD CENTER!
GOOD SHOOTING, HENRY!
...SHOT, HENRY.
UH...OH, I'M SORRY, DEX! WHAT DID YOU SAY?
MY DRINK... IT'S GONE. I SAID I COULD USE ANOTHER SHOT...
BE RIGHT THERE, DEX!
HERE YOU GO, DEX...
THANKS, HENRY... I NEED THIS! THAT THING... MY GOD... IT EATS... AND EATS... AND EATS...!
I MEAN... LORD! TWO HUMAN BEINGS... JUST GONE! ERASED! WIPED OFF... THE... FACE... OF... zzz
SORRY I HAD TO DO THAT, DEX, BUT I NEED YOU ASLEEP AND OUT OF THE WAY FOR THE NEXT FEW HOURS... YOU SEE, OLD FRIEND...
...THERE'S SO MUCH TO DO!
A SHORT TIME LATER, AT AMBERSON HALL...
YOU WERE WRONG, DEX... MIKE AND CHARLIE WEREN'T ERASED! NOT COMPLETELY... NOT YET...
HAVE TO GET STARTED... WILMA WILL BE GETTING HOME ANY TIME, NOW... SHE'LL FIND THE...

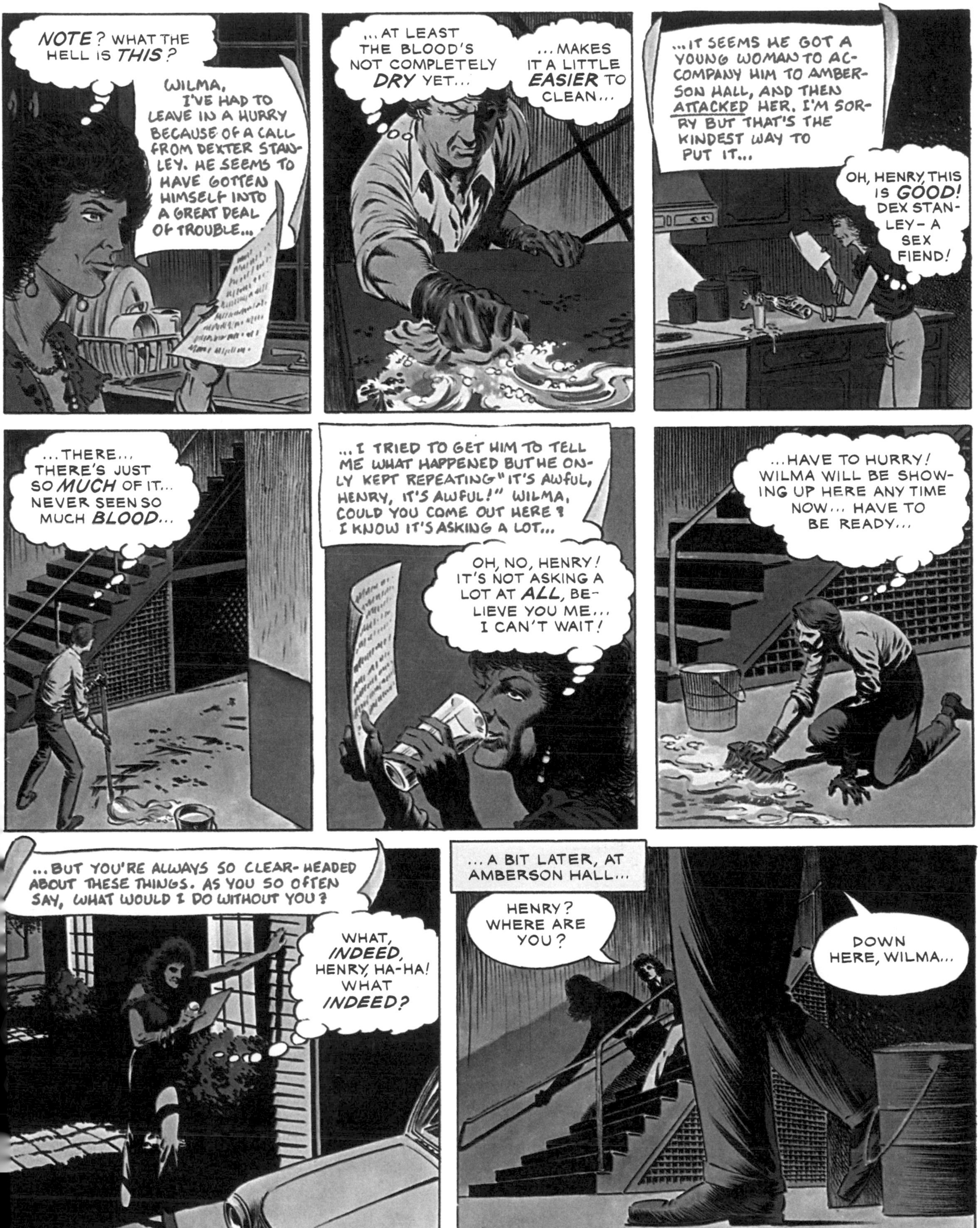
NOTE? WHAT THE HELL IS THIS?
WILMA, I'VE HAD TO LEAVE IN A HURRY BECAUSE OF A CALL FROM DEXTER STANLEY. HE SEEMS TO HAVE GOTTEN HIMSELF INTO A GREAT DEAL OF TROUBLE...
...AT LEAST THE BLOOD'S NOT COMPLETELY DRY YET...
...MAKES IT A LITTLE EASIER TO CLEAN...
...IT SEEMS HE GOT A YOUNG WOMAN TO ACCOMPANY HIM TO AMBERSON HALL, AND THEN ATTACKED HER. I'M SORRY BUT THAT'S THE KINDEST WAY TO PUT IT...
OH, HENRY, THIS IS GOOD! DEX STANLEY– A SEX FIEND!
...THERE... THERE'S JUST SO MUCH OF IT... NEVER SEEN SO MUCH BLOOD...
...I TRIED TO GET HIM TO TELL ME WHAT HAPPENED BUT HE ONLY KEPT REPEATING "IT'S AWFUL, HENRY, IT'S AWFUL!" WILMA, COULD YOU COME OUT HERE? I KNOW IT'S ASKING A LOT...
OH, NO, HENRY! IT'S NOT ASKING A LOT AT ALL, BELIEVE YOU ME... I CAN'T WAIT!
...HAVE TO HURRY! WILMA WILL BE SHOWING UP HERE ANY TIME NOW... HAVE TO BE READY...
...BUT YOU'RE ALWAYS SO CLEAR-HEADED ABOUT THESE THINGS. AS YOU SO OFTEN SAY, WHAT WOULD I DO WITHOUT YOU?
WHAT, INDEED, HENRY, HA-HA! WHAT INDEED?
...A BIT LATER, AT AMBERSON HALL...
HENRY? WHERE ARE YOU?
DOWN HERE, WILMA...

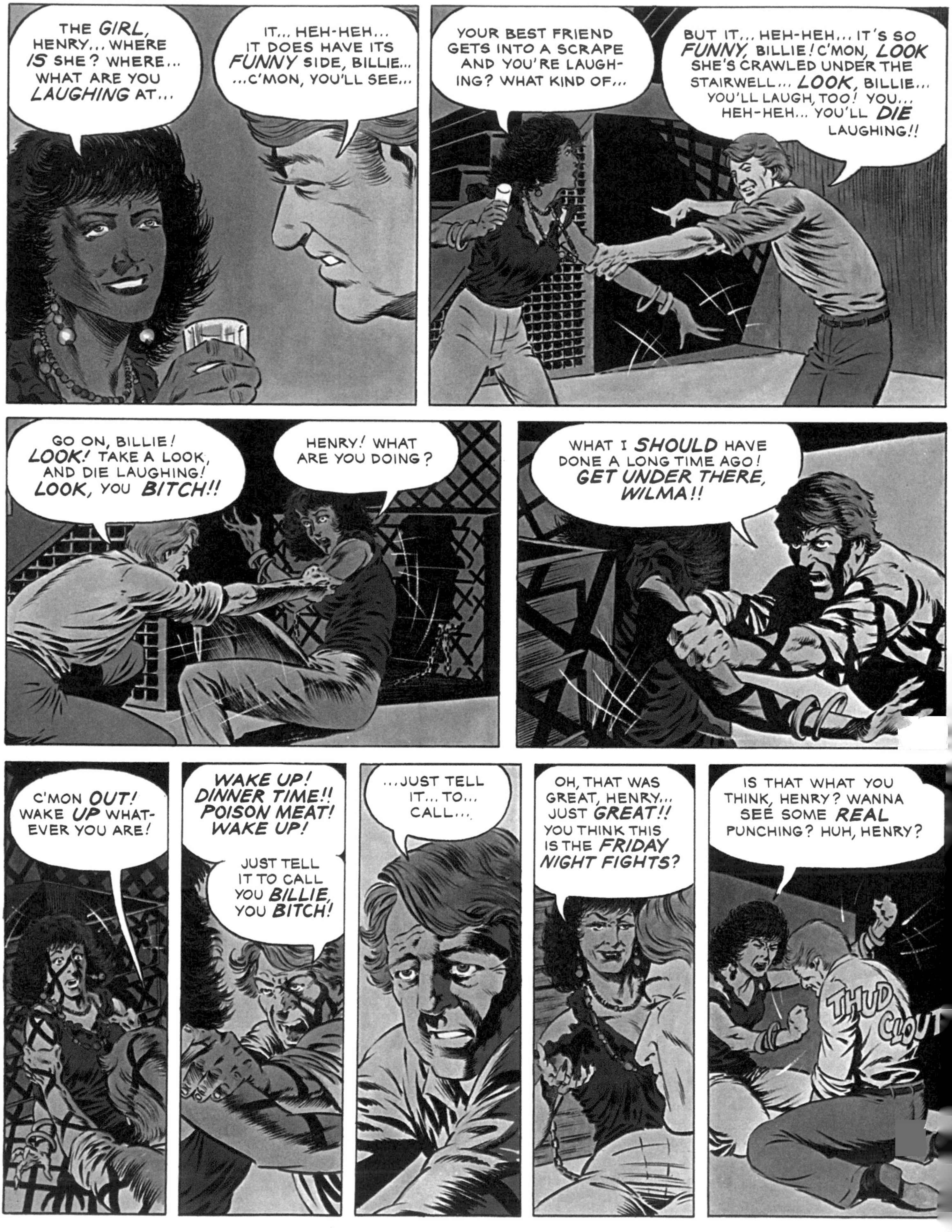
THE GIRL, HENRY... WHERE IS SHE? WHERE... WHAT ARE YOU LAUGHING AT...
IT... HEH-HEH... IT DOES HAVE ITS FUNNY SIDE, BILLIE... ...C'MON, YOU'LL SEE...
YOUR BEST FRIEND GETS INTO A SCRAPE AND YOU'RE LAUGHING? WHAT KIND OF...
BUT IT... HEH-HEH... IT'S SO FUNNY, BILLIE! C'MON, LOOK SHE'S CRAWLED UNDER THE STAIRWELL... LOOK, BILLIE... YOU'LL LAUGH, TOO! YOU... HEH-HEH... YOU'LL DIE LAUGHING!!
GO ON, BILLIE! LOOK! TAKE A LOOK, AND DIE LAUGHING! LOOK, YOU BITCH!!
HENRY! WHAT ARE YOU DOING?
WHAT I SHOULD HAVE DONE A LONG TIME AGO! GET UNDER THERE, WILMA!!
C'MON OUT! WAKE UP WHATEVER YOU ARE!
WAKE UP! DINNER TIME!! POISON MEAT! WAKE UP!
JUST TELL IT TO CALL YOU BILLIE, YOU BITCH!
...JUST TELL IT... TO... CALL...
OH, THAT WAS GREAT, HENRY... JUST GREAT!! YOU THINK THIS IS THE FRIDAY NIGHT FIGHTS?
IS THAT WHAT YOU THINK, HENRY? WANNA SEE SOME REAL PUNCHING? HUH, HENRY?
THUD
CLOUT

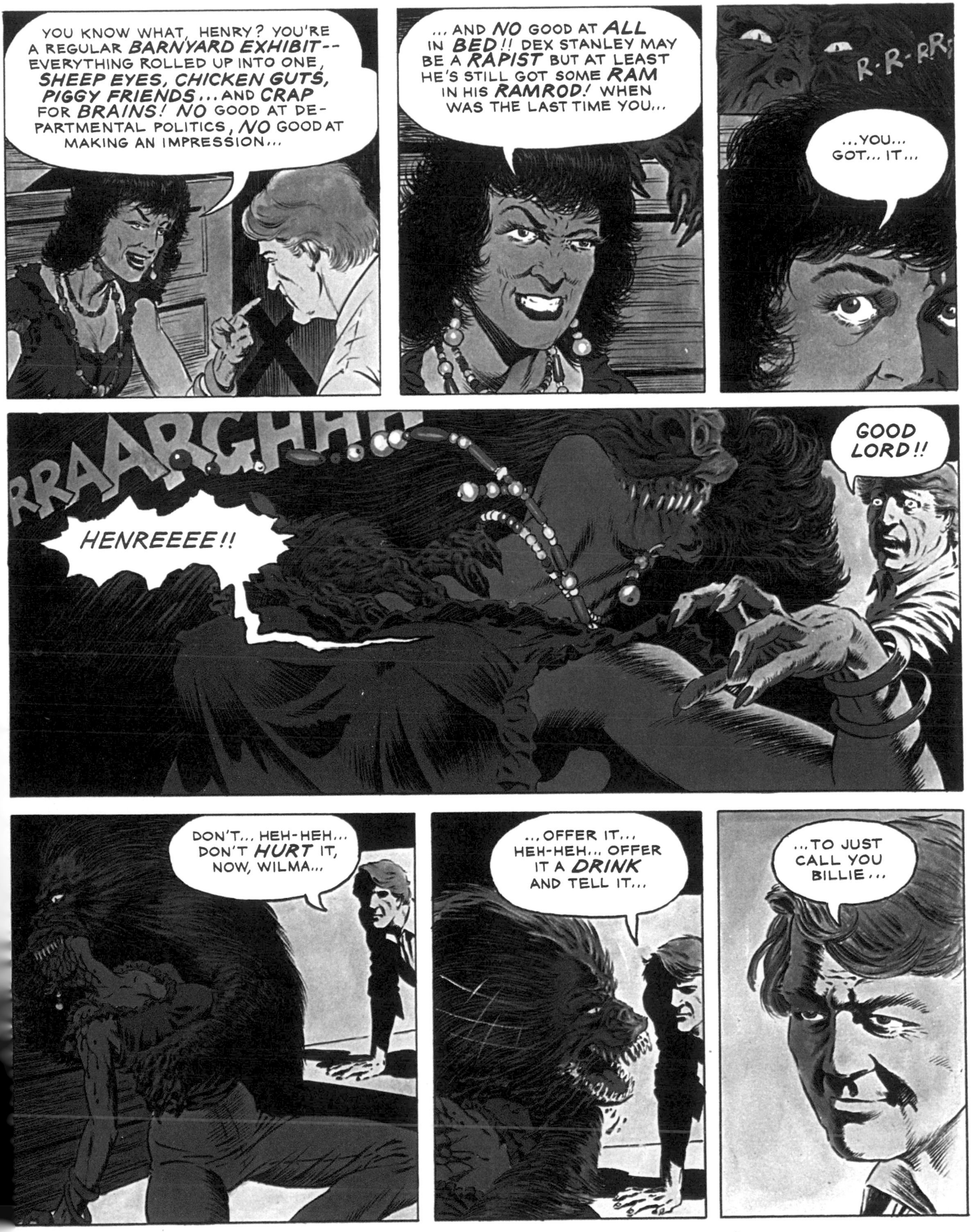
YOU KNOW WHAT, HENRY? YOU'RE A REGULAR BARNYARD EXHIBIT-- EVERYTHING ROLLED UP INTO ONE, SHEEP EYES, CHICKEN GUTS, PIGGY FRIENDS... AND CRAP FOR BRAINS! NO GOOD AT DE-PARTMENTAL POLITICS, NO GOOD AT MAKING AN IMPRESSION...
...AND NO GOOD AT ALL IN BED!! DEX STANLEY MAY BE A RAPIST BUT AT LEAST HE'S STILL GOT SOME RAM IN HIS RAMROD! WHEN WAS THE LAST TIME YOU...
R-R-RR
...YOU... GOT... IT...
RRAARGHH
HENREEEE!!
GOOD LORD!!
DON'T... HEH-HEH... DON'T HURT IT, NOW, WILMA...
...OFFER IT... HEH-HEH... OFFER IT A DRINK AND TELL IT...
...TO JUST CALL YOU BILLIE...

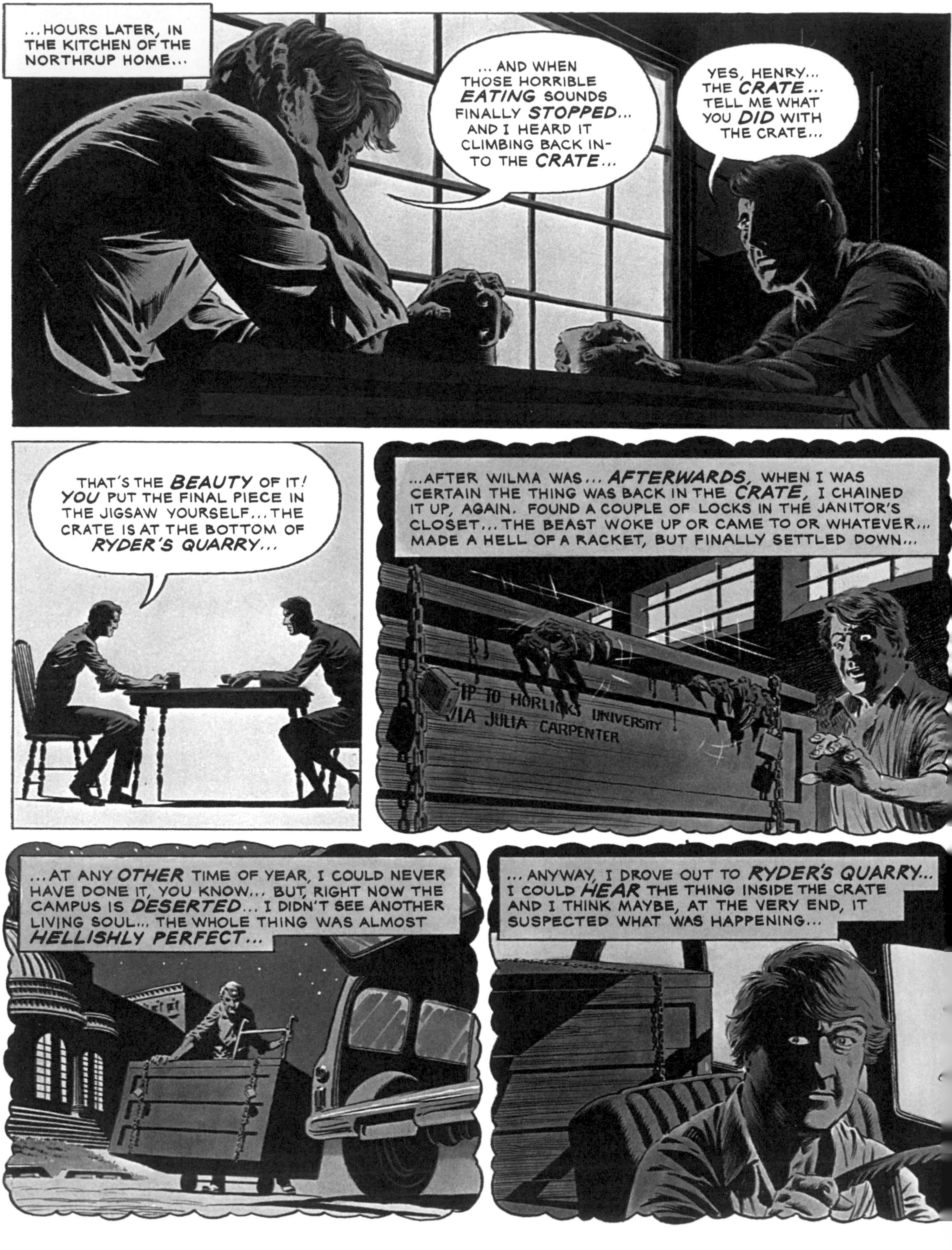
...HOURS LATER, IN THE KITCHEN OF THE NORTHRUP HOME...
...AND WHEN THOSE HORRIBLE EATING SOUNDS FINALLY STOPPED... AND I HEARD IT CLIMBING BACK INTO THE CRATE...
YES, HENRY... THE CRATE... TELL ME WHAT YOU DID WITH THE CRATE...
THAT'S THE BEAUTY OF IT! YOU PUT THE FINAL PIECE IN THE JIGSAW YOURSELF... THE CRATE IS AT THE BOTTOM OF RYDER'S QUARRY...
...AFTER WILMA WAS... AFTERWARDS, WHEN I WAS CERTAIN THE THING WAS BACK IN THE CRATE, I CHAINED IT UP, AGAIN. FOUND A COUPLE OF LOCKS IN THE JANITOR'S CLOSET... THE BEAST WOKE UP OR CAME TO OR WHATEVER... MADE A HELL OF A RACKET, BUT FINALLY SETTLED DOWN...
IP TO HORLICKS UNIVERSITY
VIA JULIA CARPENTER
...AT ANY OTHER TIME OF YEAR, I COULD NEVER HAVE DONE IT, YOU KNOW... BUT, RIGHT NOW THE CAMPUS IS DESERTED... I DIDN'T SEE ANOTHER LIVING SOUL... THE WHOLE THING WAS ALMOST HELLISHLY PERFECT...
...ANYWAY, I DROVE OUT TO RYDER'S QUARRY... I COULD HEAR THE THING INSIDE THE CRATE AND I THINK MAYBE, AT THE VERY END, IT SUSPECTED WHAT WAS HAPPENING...

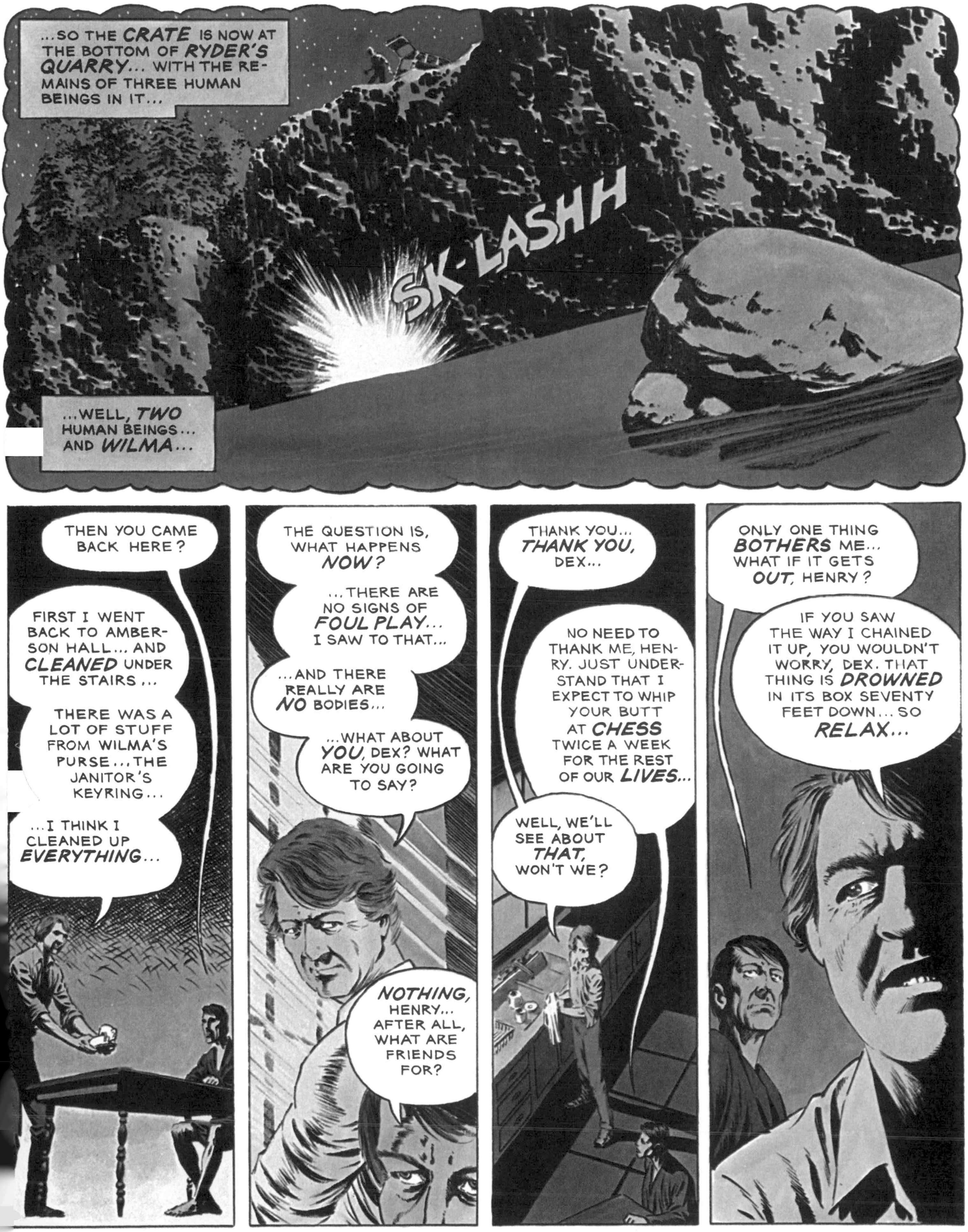
...SO THE CRATE IS NOW AT THE BOTTOM OF RYDER'S QUARRY... WITH THE REMAINS OF THREE HUMAN BEINGS IN IT...
SK-LASHH
...WELL, TWO HUMAN BEINGS... AND WILMA...
THEN YOU CAME BACK HERE?
FIRST I WENT BACK TO AMBERSON HALL... AND CLEANED UNDER THE STAIRS...
THERE WAS A LOT OF STUFF FROM WILMA'S PURSE... THE JANITOR'S KEYRING...
...I THINK I CLEANED UP EVERYTHING...
THE QUESTION IS, WHAT HAPPENS NOW?
...THERE ARE NO SIGNS OF FOUL PLAY... I SAW TO THAT...
...AND THERE REALLY ARE NO BODIES...
...WHAT ABOUT YOU, DEX? WHAT ARE YOU GOING TO SAY?
NOTHING, HENRY... AFTER ALL, WHAT ARE FRIENDS FOR?
THANK YOU... THANK YOU, DEX...
NO NEED TO THANK ME, HENRY. JUST UNDERSTAND THAT I EXPECT TO WHIP YOUR BUTT AT CHESS TWICE A WEEK FOR THE REST OF OUR LIVES...
WELL, WE'LL SEE ABOUT THAT, WON'T WE?
ONLY ONE THING BOTHERS ME... WHAT IF IT GETS OUT, HENRY?
IF YOU SAW THE WAY I CHAINED IT UP, YOU WOULDN'T WORRY, DEX. THAT THING IS DROWNED IN ITS BOX SEVENTY FEET DOWN... SO RELAX...

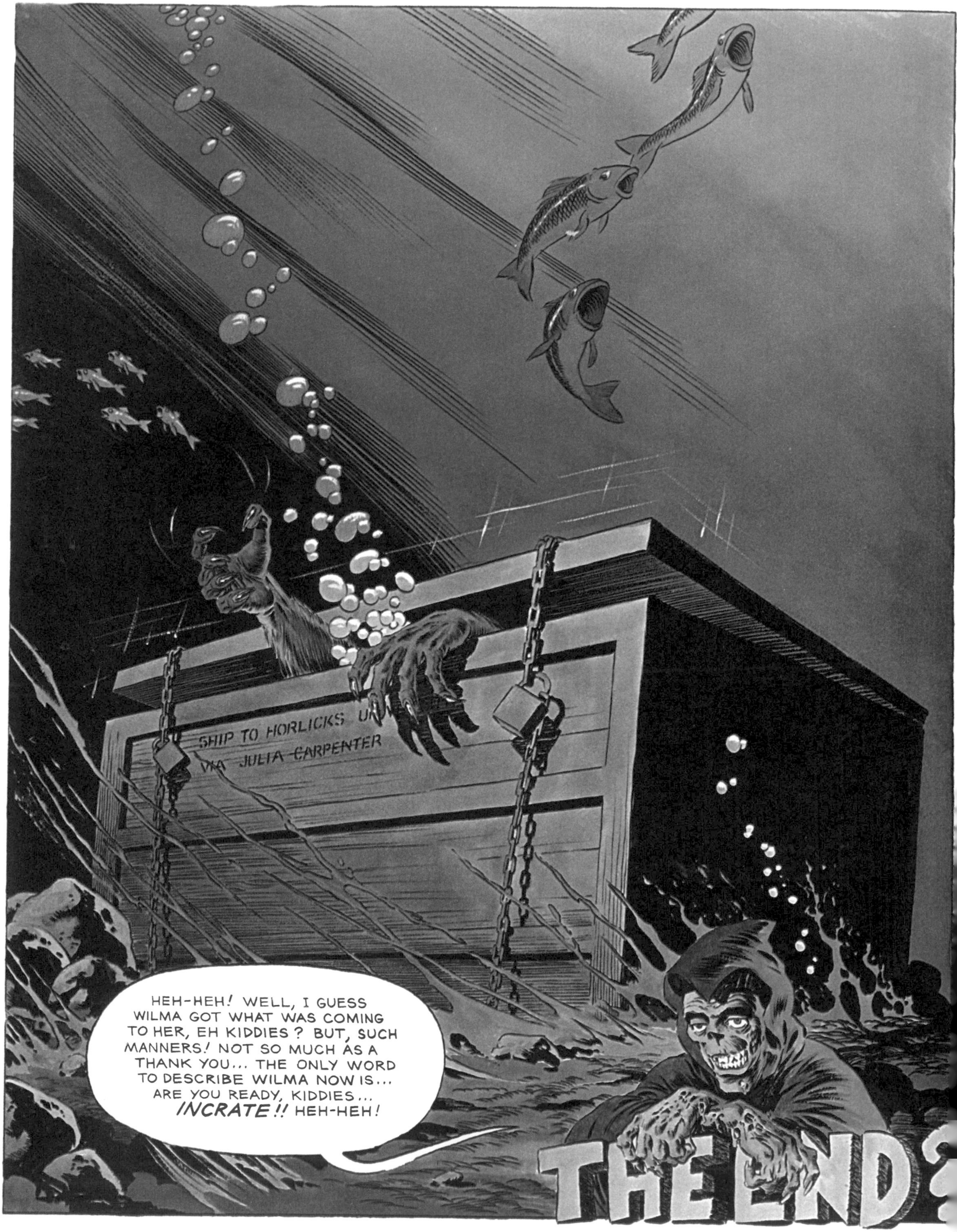
SHIP TO HORLICKS U
VIA JULIA CARPENTER
HEH-HEH! WELL, I GUESS WILMA GOT WHAT WAS COMING TO HER, EH KIDDIES? BUT, SUCH MANNERS! NOT SO MUCH AS A THANK YOU... THE ONLY WORD TO DESCRIBE WILMA NOW IS... ARE YOU READY, KIDDIES... INCRATE!! HEH-HEH!
THE END?

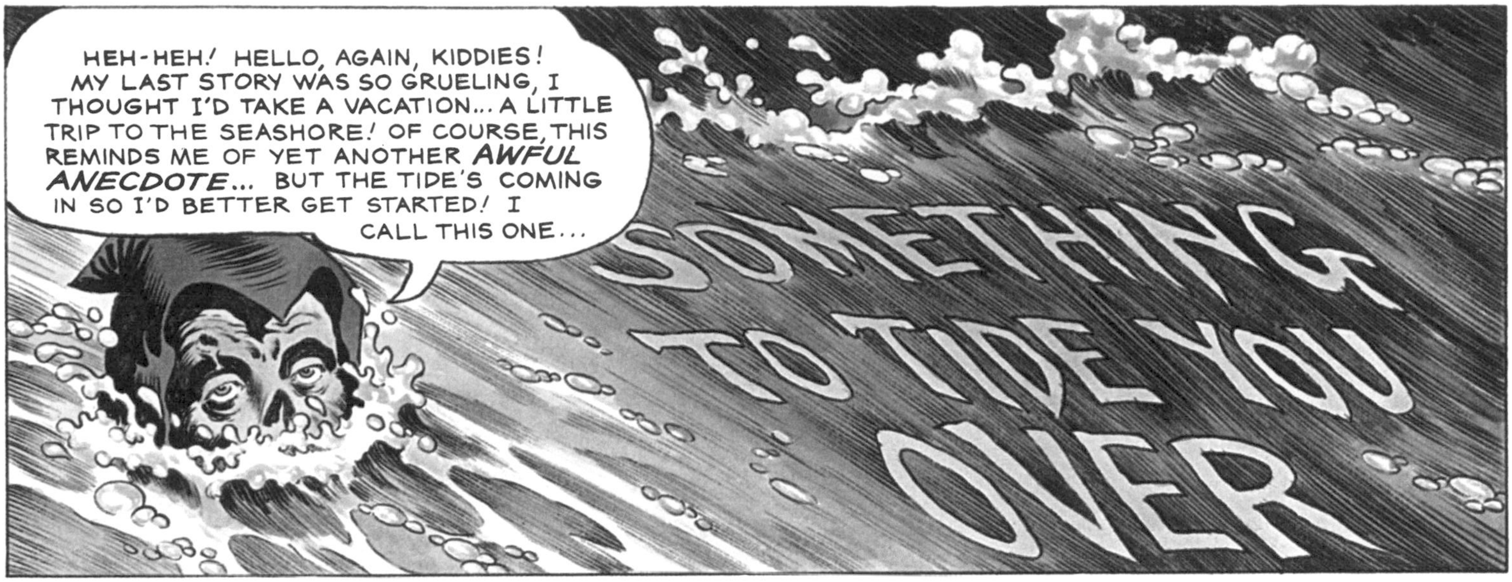
HEH-HEH! HELLO, AGAIN, KIDDIES! MY LAST STORY WAS SO GRUELING, I THOUGHT I'D TAKE A VACATION... A LITTLE TRIP TO THE SEASHORE! OF COURSE, THIS REMINDS ME OF YET ANOTHER AWFUL ANECDOTE... BUT THE TIDE'S COMING IN SO I'D BETTER GET STARTED! I CALL THIS ONE...
SOMETHING TO TIDE YOU OVER

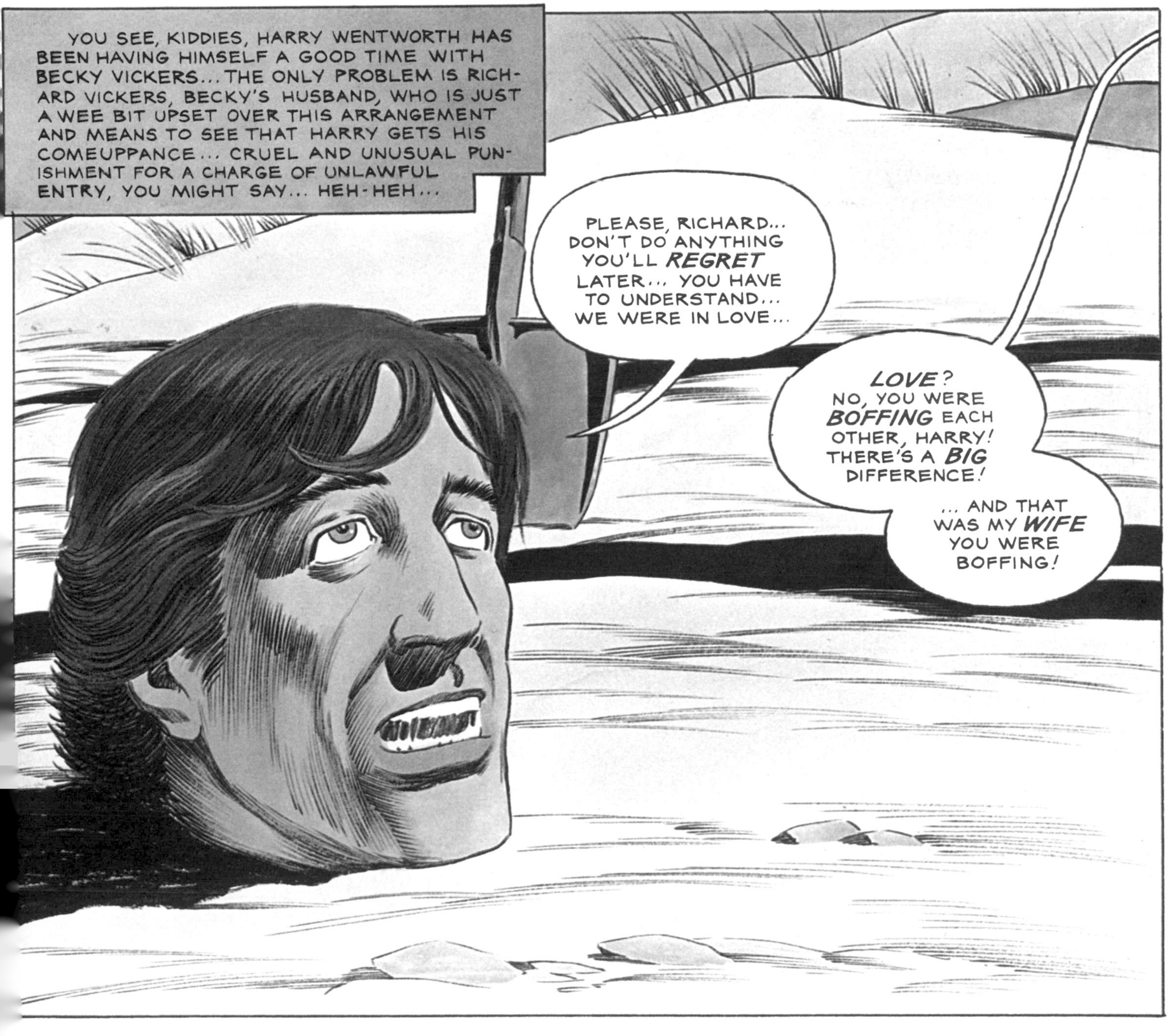
YOU SEE, KIDDIES, HARRY WENTWORTH HAS BEEN HAVING HIMSELF A GOOD TIME WITH BECKY VICKERS... THE ONLY PROBLEM IS RICHARD VICKERS, BECKY'S HUSBAND, WHO IS JUST A WEE BIT UPSET OVER THIS ARRANGEMENT AND MEANS TO SEE THAT HARRY GETS HIS COMEUPPANCE... CRUEL AND UNUSUAL PUNISHMENT FOR A CHARGE OF UNLAWFUL ENTRY, YOU MIGHT SAY... HEH-HEH...
PLEASE, RICHARD... DON'T DO ANYTHING YOU'LL REGRET LATER... YOU HAVE TO UNDERSTAND... WE WERE IN LOVE...
LOVE? NO, YOU WERE BOFFING EACH OTHER, HARRY! THERE'S A BIG DIFFERENCE!
... AND THAT WAS MY WIFE YOU WERE BOFFING!

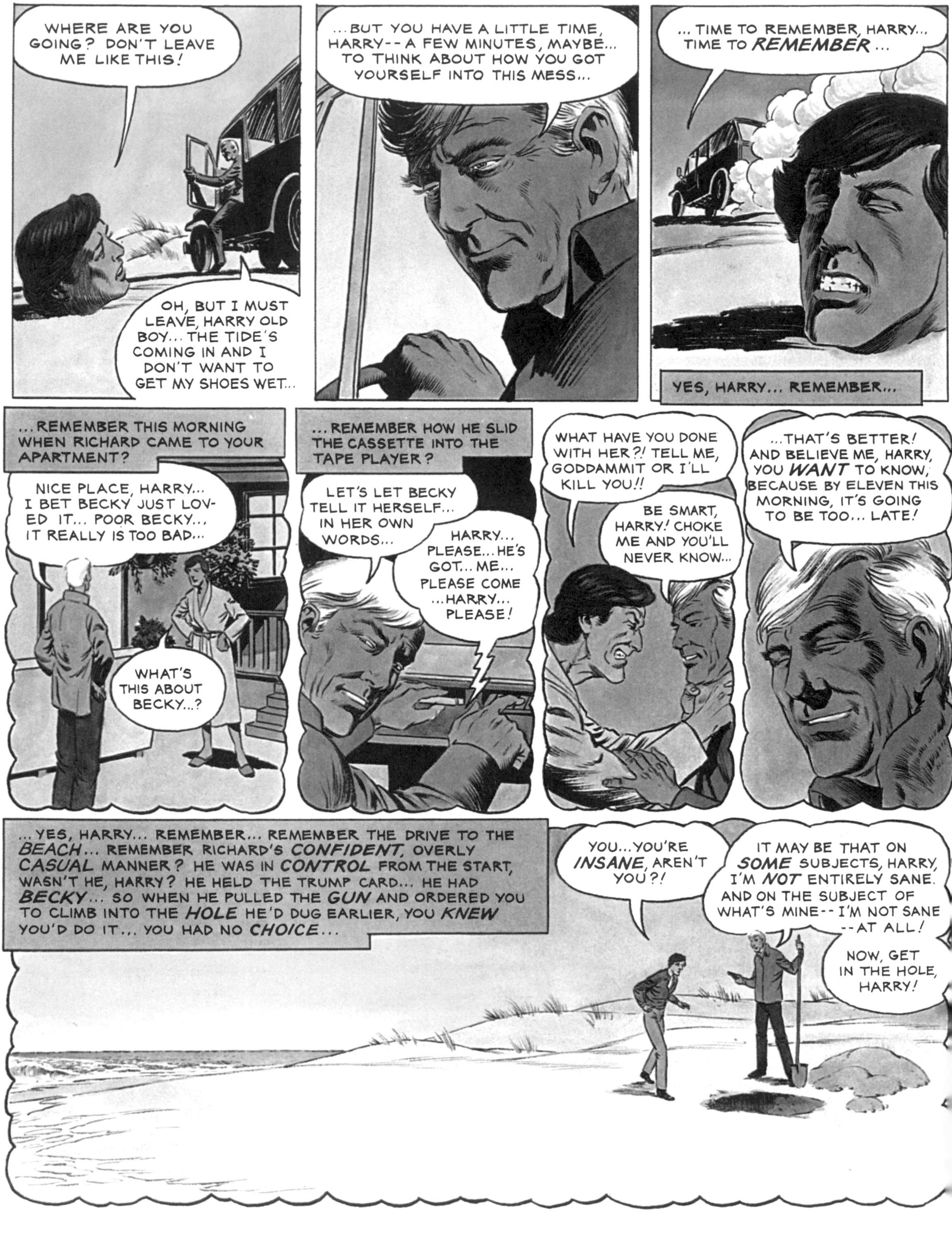
WHERE ARE YOU GOING? DON'T LEAVE ME LIKE THIS!
OH, BUT I MUST LEAVE, HARRY OLD BOY... THE TIDE'S COMING IN AND I DON'T WANT TO GET MY SHOES WET...
...BUT YOU HAVE A LITTLE TIME, HARRY-- A FEW MINUTES, MAYBE... TO THINK ABOUT HOW YOU GOT YOURSELF INTO THIS MESS...
... TIME TO REMEMBER, HARRY... TIME TO REMEMBER...
YES, HARRY... REMEMBER...
...REMEMBER THIS MORNING WHEN RICHARD CAME TO YOUR APARTMENT?
NICE PLACE, HARRY... I BET BECKY JUST LOVED IT... POOR BECKY... IT REALLY IS TOO BAD...
WHAT'S THIS ABOUT BECKY...?
...REMEMBER HOW HE SLID THE CASSETTE INTO THE TAPE PLAYER?
LET'S LET BECKY TELL IT HERSELF... IN HER OWN WORDS...
HARRY... PLEASE... HE'S GOT... ME... PLEASE COME ...HARRY... PLEASE!
WHAT HAVE YOU DONE WITH HER?! TELL ME, GODDAMMIT OR I'LL KILL YOU!!
BE SMART, HARRY! CHOKE ME AND YOU'LL NEVER KNOW...
...THAT'S BETTER! AND BELIEVE ME, HARRY, YOU WANT TO KNOW, BECAUSE BY ELEVEN THIS MORNING, IT'S GOING TO BE TOO... LATE!
...YES, HARRY... REMEMBER... REMEMBER THE DRIVE TO THE BEACH... REMEMBER RICHARD'S CONFIDENT, OVERLY CASUAL MANNER? HE WAS IN CONTROL FROM THE START, WASN'T HE, HARRY? HE HELD THE TRUMP CARD... HE HAD BECKY... SO WHEN HE PULLED THE GUN AND ORDERED YOU TO CLIMB INTO THE HOLE HE'D DUG EARLIER, YOU KNEW YOU'D DO IT... YOU HAD NO CHOICE...
YOU...YOU'RE INSANE, AREN'T YOU?!
IT MAY BE THAT ON SOME SUBJECTS, HARRY, I'M NOT ENTIRELY SANE. AND ON THE SUBJECT OF WHAT'S MINE-- I'M NOT SANE --AT ALL!
NOW, GET IN THE HOLE, HARRY!

YOU KEPT THINKING IT WOULD *END*, DIDN'T YOU, HARRY-BOY?

VERY GOOD, HARRY! NOW START PULLING SAND INTO THE HOLE...

BUT IT WENT ON...

...IT'S HIP-HIGH... GOOD BOY, HARRY, GOOD BOY! NOW, HANDS IN POCKETS AND STAND VERY, *VERY STILL*...

...AND ON...

...BECAUSE IF YOU *MOVE*, JUST THE TINIEST BIT, I MIGHT HAVE TO TAKE MY SHOVEL AND SMASH YOUR GODDAMNED HEAD IN... AND I WOULD NOT WANT TO DO THAT, HARRY... OH, NO...

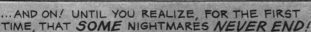

...AND ON! UNTIL YOU REALIZE, FOR THE FIRST TIME, THAT *SOME* NIGHTMARES *NEVER END!*

THERE, THAT'S GOT IT! DON'T GO AWAY, HARRY... I'LL BE RIGHT BACK...

...REMEMBER HOW WHEN HE'D FINISHED, HE TURN- ED AND WALKED AWAY?

RICHARD! DON'T GO... DON'T LEAVE ME... PLEASE...

...HOW HE'D RETURNED MOMENTS LATER, THE TV CABLE TRAILING BEHIND HIM LIKE A HUGE BLACK SNAKE?

SEE, HARRY? I TOLD YOU I'D BE RIGHT BACK...

...AND THEN, INCREDIBLY, HE'D SET UP THE TRIPOD... TOPPED BY A SMALL VIDI-CAM?

HOW'S THE ANGLE, HARRY? THAT'S IT, LOOK RIGHT INTO THE LENS... SAY CHEEEESE!

...THEN CONNEC- TED THE WIRES...

DON'T WORRY ABOUT POWER, HARRY... THIS CABLE RUNS BACK TO MY HOUSE... ABOUT A QUARTER MILE FROM HERE...

...HOW HE THEN SET UP THE MONITOR?

COMFORTABLE, HARRY? GOOD...

...REMEMBER HOW YOU SCREAMED WHEN HE SWITCHED IT ON, HARRY? SCREAMED BECAUSE OF WHAT YOU SAW??

/////IT'S SHOWTIME!!

BECKY!!

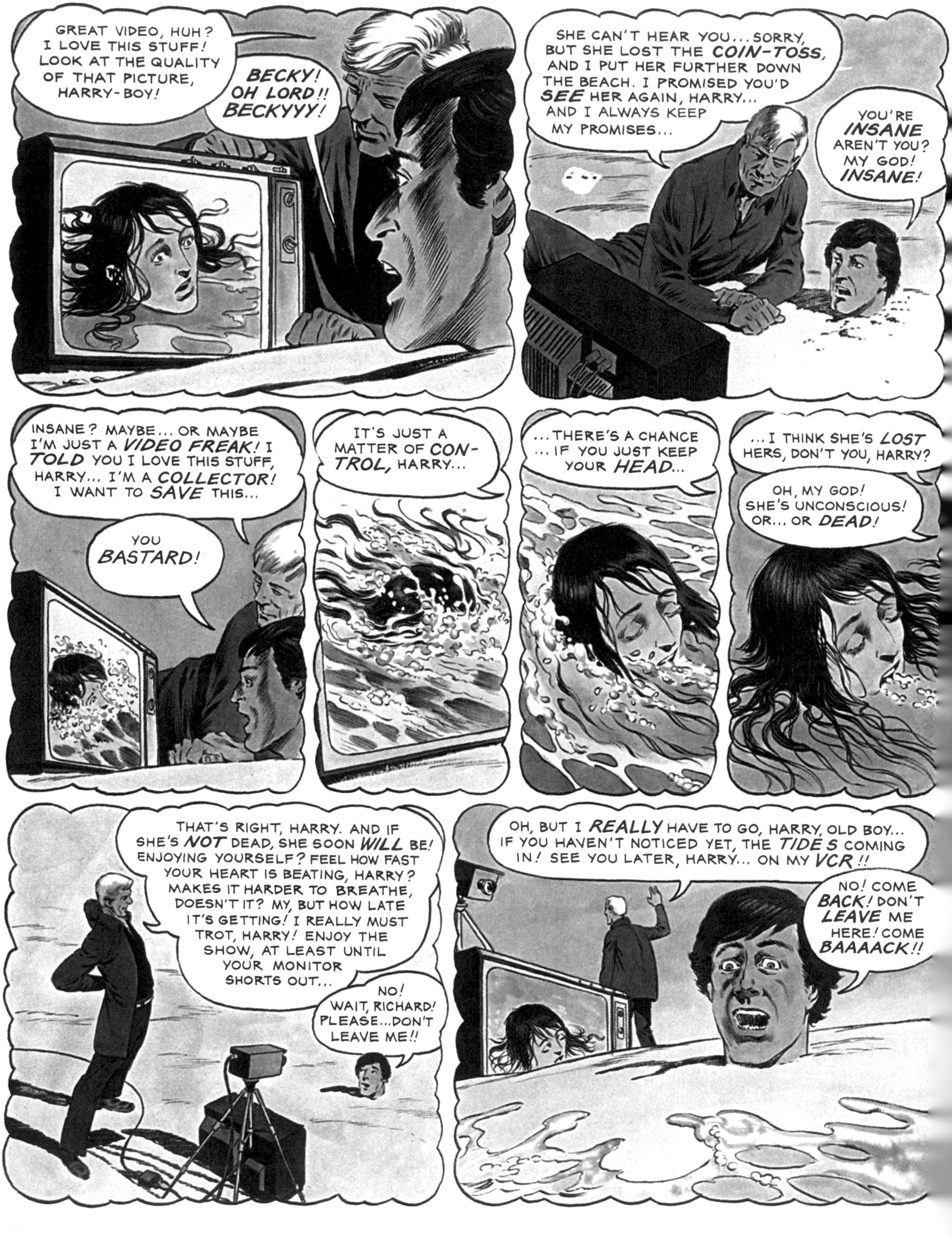
GREAT VIDEO, HUH? I LOVE THIS STUFF! LOOK AT THE QUALITY OF THAT PICTURE, HARRY-BOY!
BECKY! OH LORD!! BECKYYY!
SHE CAN'T HEAR YOU... SORRY, BUT SHE LOST THE COIN-TOSS, AND I PUT HER FURTHER DOWN THE BEACH. I PROMISED YOU'D SEE HER AGAIN, HARRY... AND I ALWAYS KEEP MY PROMISES...
YOU'RE INSANE AREN'T YOU? MY GOD! INSANE!
INSANE? MAYBE... OR MAYBE I'M JUST A VIDEO FREAK! I TOLD YOU I LOVE THIS STUFF, HARRY... I'M A COLLECTOR! I WANT TO SAVE THIS...
YOU BASTARD!
IT'S JUST A MATTER OF CON-TROL, HARRY...
...THERE'S A CHANCE ...IF YOU JUST KEEP YOUR HEAD...
...I THINK SHE'S LOST HERS, DON'T YOU, HARRY?
OH, MY GOD! SHE'S UNCONSCIOUS! OR... OR DEAD!
THAT'S RIGHT, HARRY. AND IF SHE'S NOT DEAD, SHE SOON WILL BE! ENJOYING YOURSELF? FEEL HOW FAST YOUR HEART IS BEATING, HARRY? MAKES IT HARDER TO BREATHE, DOESN'T IT? MY, BUT HOW LATE IT'S GETTING! I REALLY MUST TROT, HARRY! ENJOY THE SHOW, AT LEAST UNTIL YOUR MONITOR SHORTS OUT...
NO! WAIT, RICHARD! PLEASE...DON'T LEAVE ME!!
OH, BUT I REALLY HAVE TO GO, HARRY, OLD BOY... IF YOU HAVEN'T NOTICED YET, THE TIDE'S COMING IN! SEE YOU LATER, HARRY... ON MY VCR!!
NO! COME BACK! DON'T LEAVE ME HERE! COME BAAAACK!!

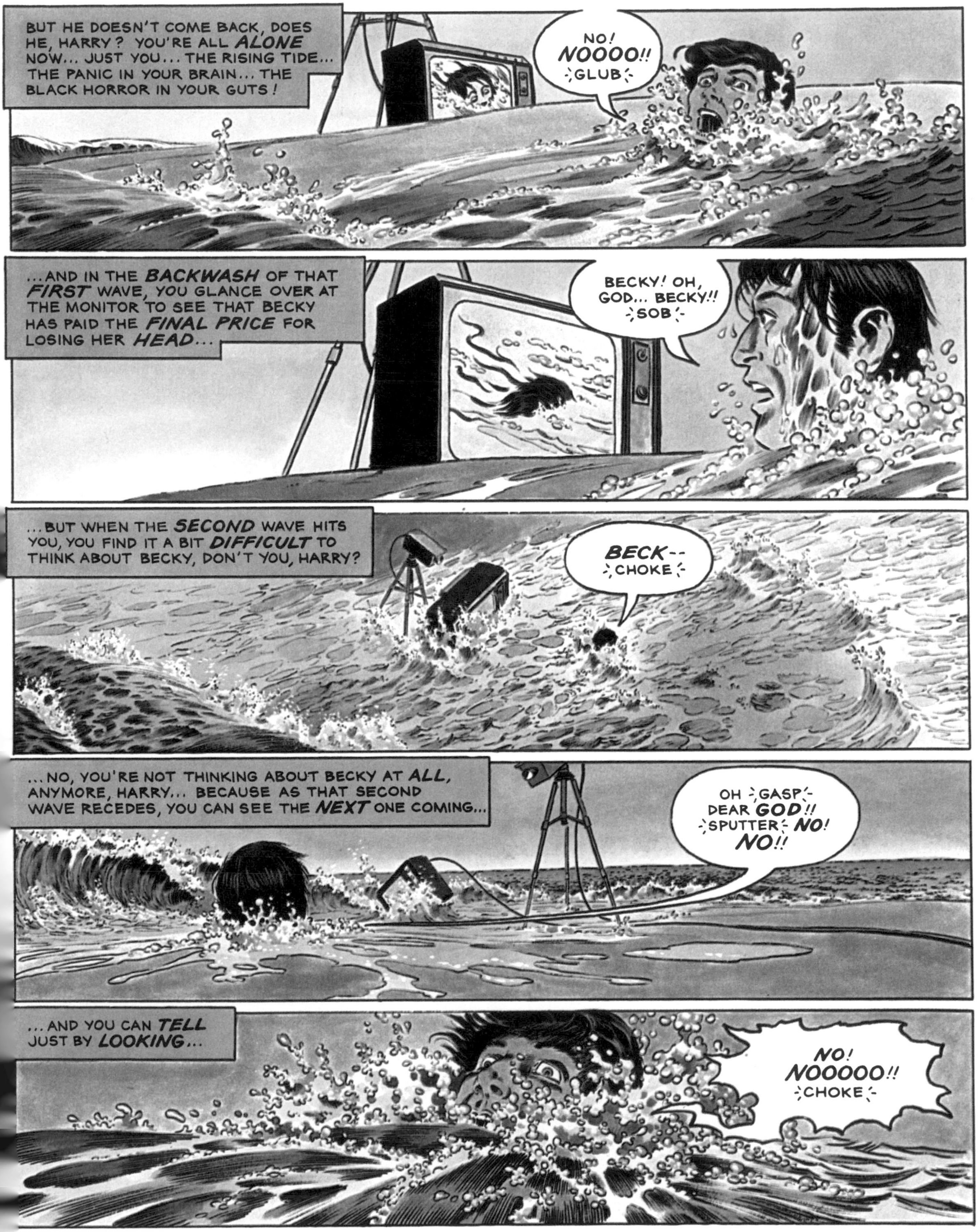
BUT HE DOESN'T COME BACK, DOES HE, HARRY? YOU'RE ALL ALONE NOW... JUST YOU... THE RISING TIDE... THE PANIC IN YOUR BRAIN... THE BLACK HORROR IN YOUR GUTS!
NO! NOOOO!! GLUB
...AND IN THE BACKWASH OF THAT FIRST WAVE, YOU GLANCE OVER AT THE MONITOR TO SEE THAT BECKY HAS PAID THE FINAL PRICE FOR LOSING HER HEAD...
BECKY! OH, GOD... BECKY!! SOB
...BUT WHEN THE SECOND WAVE HITS YOU, YOU FIND IT A BIT DIFFICULT TO THINK ABOUT BECKY, DON'T YOU, HARRY?
BECK-- CHOKE
...NO, YOU'RE NOT THINKING ABOUT BECKY AT ALL, ANYMORE, HARRY... BECAUSE AS THAT SECOND WAVE RECEDES, YOU CAN SEE THE NEXT ONE COMING...
OH GASP DEAR GOD!! SPUTTER NO! NO!!
...AND YOU CAN TELL JUST BY LOOKING...
NO! NOOOOO!! CHOKE

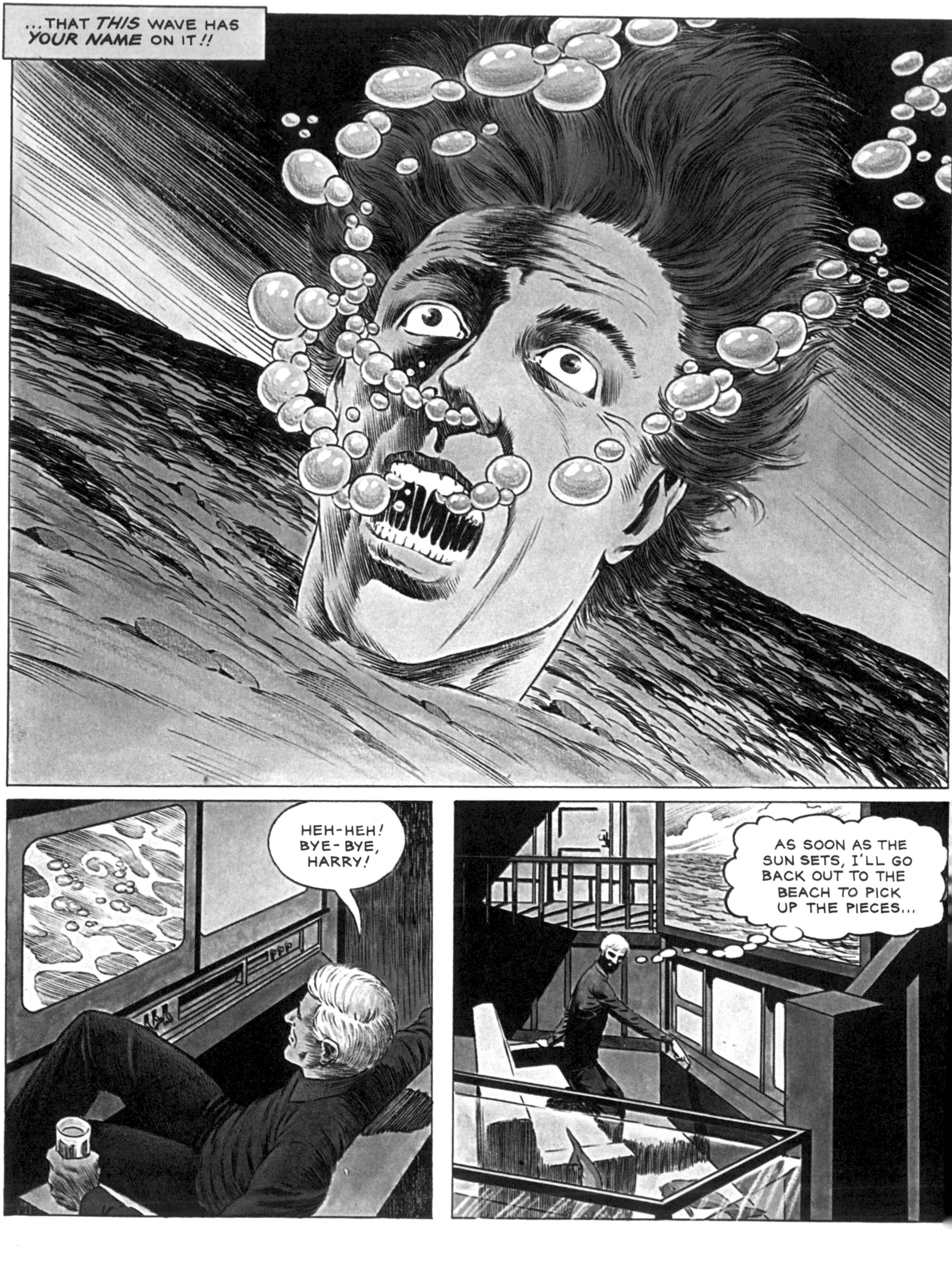
...THAT *THIS* WAVE HAS *YOUR NAME* ON IT!!
HEH-HEH! BYE-BYE, HARRY!
AS SOON AS THE SUN SETS, I'LL GO BACK OUT TO THE BEACH TO PICK UP THE PIECES...

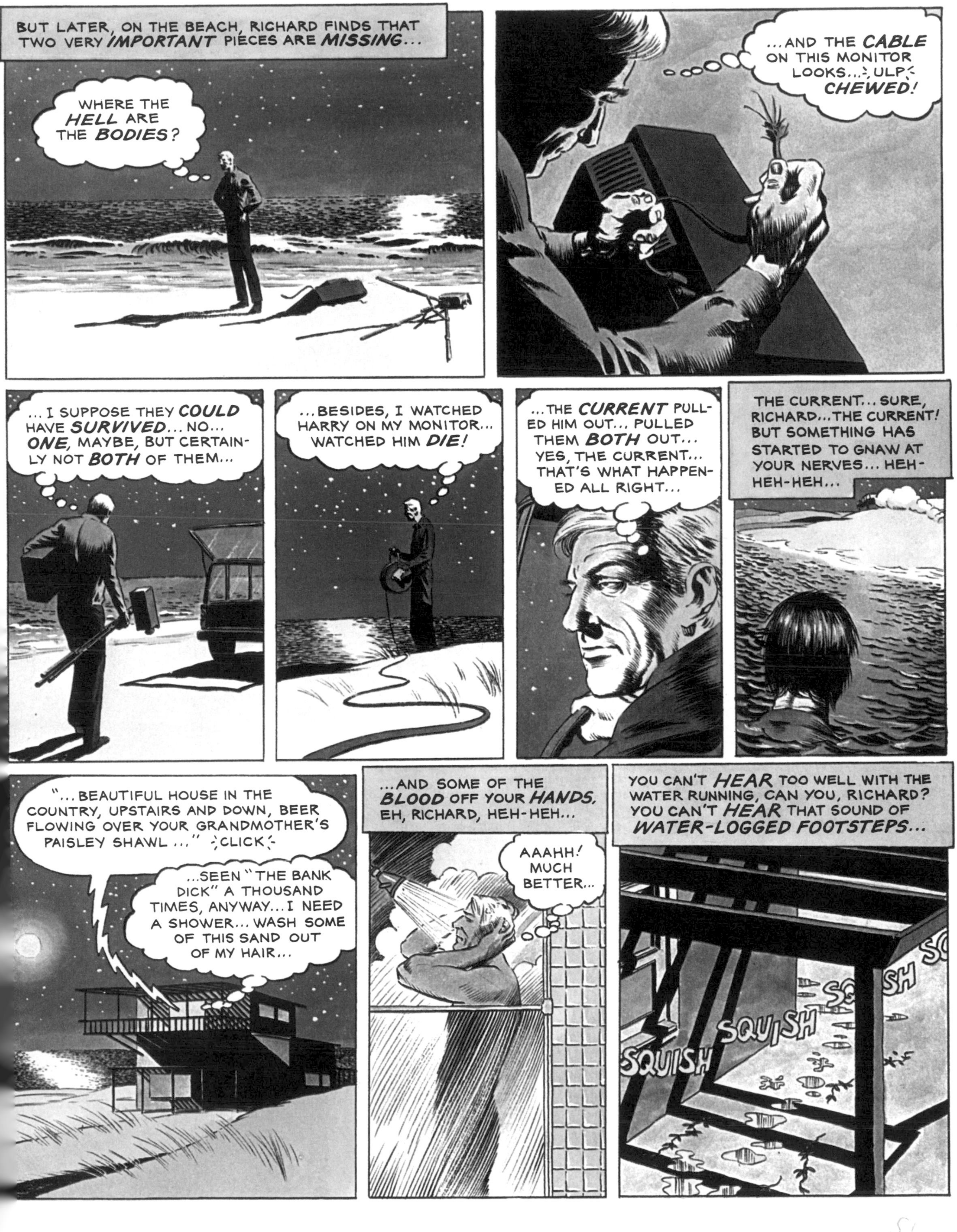
BUT LATER, ON THE BEACH, RICHARD FINDS THAT TWO VERY IMPORTANT PIECES ARE MISSING...
WHERE THE HELL ARE THE BODIES?
...AND THE CABLE ON THIS MONITOR LOOKS... ULP CHEWED!
...I SUPPOSE THEY COULD HAVE SURVIVED... NO... ONE, MAYBE, BUT CERTAINLY NOT BOTH OF THEM...
...BESIDES, I WATCHED HARRY ON MY MONITOR... WATCHED HIM DIE!
...THE CURRENT PULLED HIM OUT... PULLED THEM BOTH OUT... YES, THE CURRENT... THAT'S WHAT HAPPENED ALL RIGHT...
THE CURRENT... SURE, RICHARD... THE CURRENT! BUT SOMETHING HAS STARTED TO GNAW AT YOUR NERVES... HEH-HEH-HEH...
"...BEAUTIFUL HOUSE IN THE COUNTRY, UPSTAIRS AND DOWN, BEER FLOWING OVER YOUR GRANDMOTHER'S PAISLEY SHAWL ..." CLICK
...SEEN "THE BANK DICK" A THOUSAND TIMES, ANYWAY... I NEED A SHOWER... WASH SOME OF THIS SAND OUT OF MY HAIR...
...AND SOME OF THE BLOOD OFF YOUR HANDS, EH, RICHARD, HEH-HEH...
AAAHH! MUCH BETTER...
YOU CAN'T HEAR TOO WELL WITH THE WATER RUNNING, CAN YOU, RICHARD? YOU CAN'T HEAR THAT SOUND OF WATER-LOGGED FOOTSTEPS...
SQUISH
SQUISH
SQUISH
SQUISH

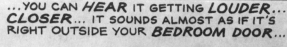

Panel 1:
...BUT YOU CAN *SMELL* IT, CAN'T YOU, RICHARD? THAT AWFUL LOW-TIDE *STENCH* UNDERLAID WITH...SOMETHING *ELSE*?

WHAT THE...?

Panel 2:
TURN OFF THE WATER, RICHARD! AHH, *NOW* YOU CAN *HEAR* IT...

IS THAT *YOU*, WENTWORTH?

SQUISH DRIP DRIP SKSH SQUISH

Panel 3:
...YOU CAN *HEAR* IT GETTING *LOUDER*... *CLOSER*... IT SOUNDS ALMOST AS IF IT'S RIGHT OUTSIDE YOUR *BEDROOM DOOR*...

MAY I SUGGEST THAT YOU DON'T COME IN HERE?

SQUISH SKISH SQUISH DRIP DRIP

Panel 4:
I'VE GOT THE *GUN*, DEAR BOY, AND BELIEVE ME, I'LL USE IT...

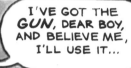
SH SQUISH

Panel 5:
I'LL SHOOT YOU DEA-- *GOOD LORD!!*

YOU CAN'T SHOOT US DEAD, RICHARD...

...BECAUSE WE'RE ALREADY DEAD...

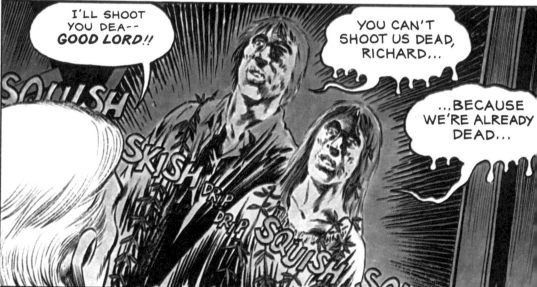

SQUISH SKISH DRIP DRIP SQUISH

Panel 6:
THEY'RE COMING *CLOSER* RICHARD! *DO* SOMETHING!

ALREADY DEAD, RICHARD...

...ALREADY...

BAM SQUISH SKISH

Panel 7:
HEH-HEH! *NOW* DO SOMETHING *ELSE*...

...DEAD, RICHARD...

DRIP SQUISH SQUISH

Panel 8:
...OKAY, RICHARD! IF THE *BULLETS* DON'T STOP THEM...

ALREADY DEAD...

BAM BAM SQUISH CLICK

Panel 9:
...WHY NOT TRY *THROWING* THE GUN? OH, THAT'S A *BIIIG* HELP, RICHARD... *VERY* SMART!

ALREADY DEAD, RICHARD...

...ALREADY DEAD...

NO! KEEP AWAY!

THUD SQUISH DRIP DRIP SKISH

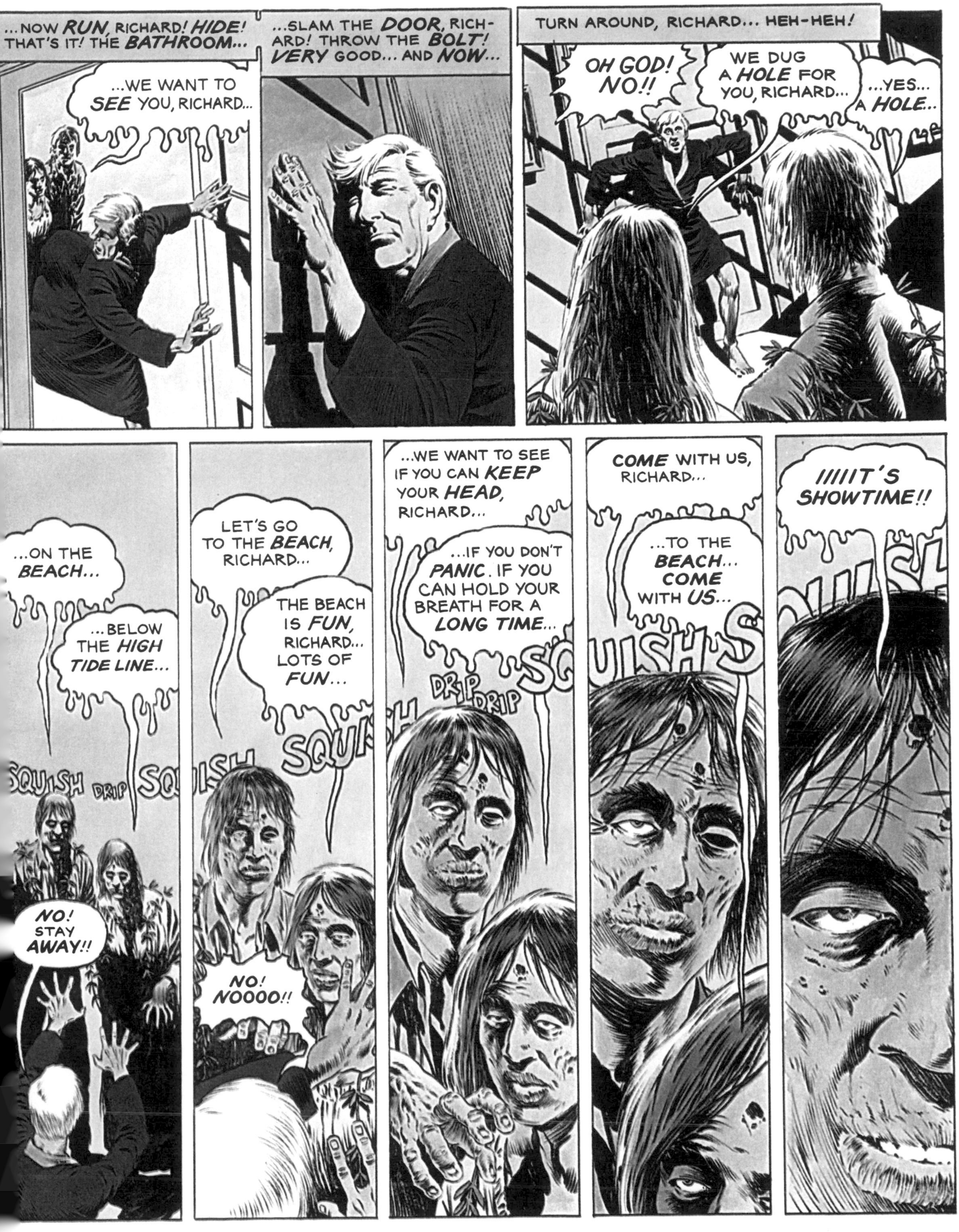

...NOW RUN, RICHARD! HIDE! THAT'S IT! THE BATHROOM...
...WE WANT TO SEE YOU, RICHARD...
...SLAM THE DOOR, RICHARD! THROW THE BOLT! VERY GOOD... AND NOW...
TURN AROUND, RICHARD... HEH-HEH!
OH GOD! NO!!
WE DUG A HOLE FOR YOU, RICHARD...
...YES... A HOLE...
...ON THE BEACH...
...BELOW THE HIGH TIDE LINE...
SQUISH DRIP SQUISH
NO! STAY AWAY!!
LET'S GO TO THE BEACH, RICHARD...
THE BEACH IS FUN, RICHARD... LOTS OF FUN...
SQUISH
NO! NOOOO!!
...WE WANT TO SEE IF YOU CAN KEEP YOUR HEAD, RICHARD...
...IF YOU DON'T PANIC. IF YOU CAN HOLD YOUR BREATH FOR A LONG TIME...
DRIP DRIP
COME WITH US, RICHARD...
...TO THE BEACH... COME WITH US...
SQUISH SQUISH
IIIIIT'S SHOWTIME!!
SQUISH

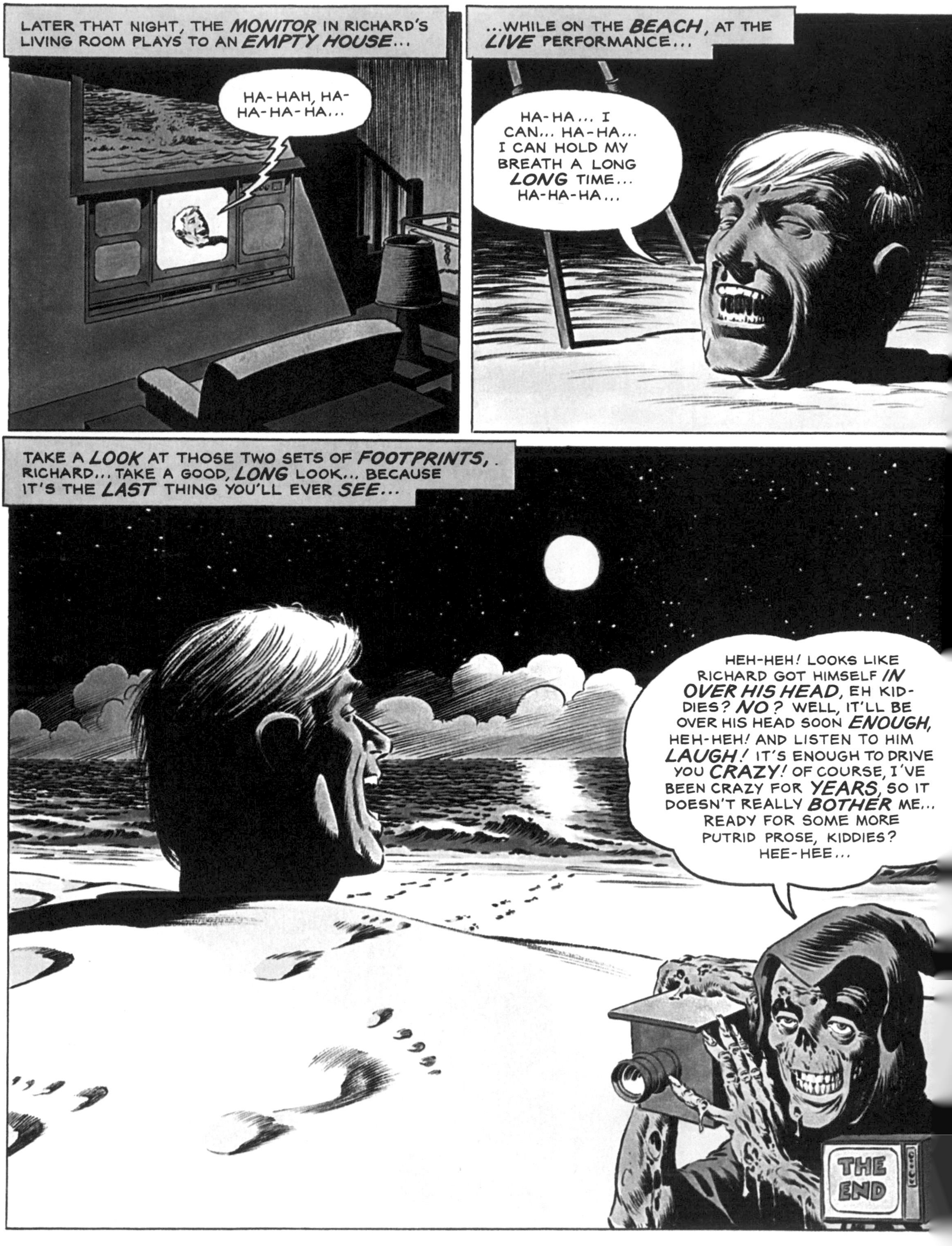
LATER THAT NIGHT, THE MONITOR IN RICHARD'S LIVING ROOM PLAYS TO AN EMPTY HOUSE...
HA-HAH, HA-HA-HA-HA...
...WHILE ON THE BEACH, AT THE LIVE PERFORMANCE...
HA-HA... I CAN... HA-HA... I CAN HOLD MY BREATH A LONG LONG TIME... HA-HA-HA...
TAKE A LOOK AT THOSE TWO SETS OF FOOTPRINTS, RICHARD... TAKE A GOOD, LONG LOOK... BECAUSE IT'S THE LAST THING YOU'LL EVER SEE...
HEH-HEH! LOOKS LIKE RICHARD GOT HIMSELF IN OVER HIS HEAD, EH KID-DIES? NO? WELL, IT'LL BE OVER HIS HEAD SOON ENOUGH, HEH-HEH! AND LISTEN TO HIM LAUGH! IT'S ENOUGH TO DRIVE YOU CRAZY! OF COURSE, I'VE BEEN CRAZY FOR YEARS, SO IT DOESN'T REALLY BOTHER ME... READY FOR SOME MORE PUTRID PROSE, KIDDIES? HEE-HEE...
THE END

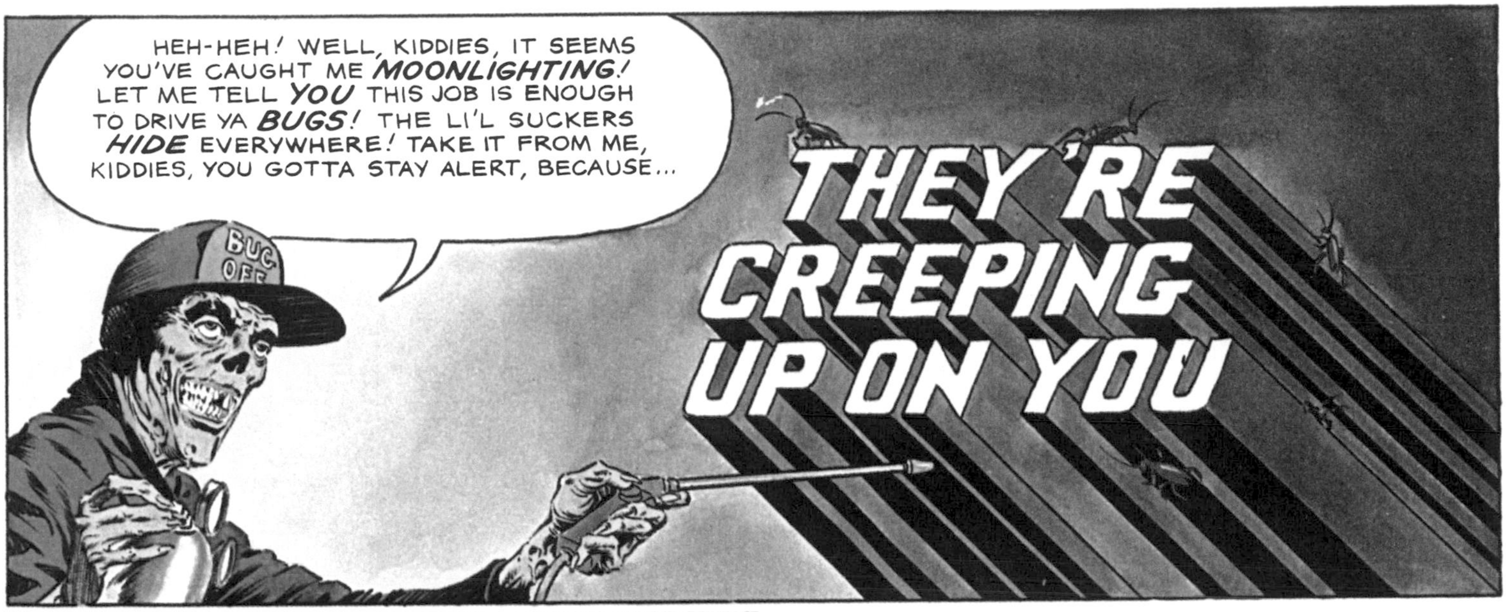
HEH-HEH! WELL, KIDDIES, IT SEEMS YOU'VE CAUGHT ME MOONLIGHTING! LET ME TELL YOU THIS JOB IS ENOUGH TO DRIVE YA BUGS! THE LI'L SUCKERS HIDE EVERYWHERE! TAKE IT FROM ME, KIDDIES, YOU GOTTA STAY ALERT, BECAUSE...
BUG OFF
THEY'RE CREEPING UP ON YOU

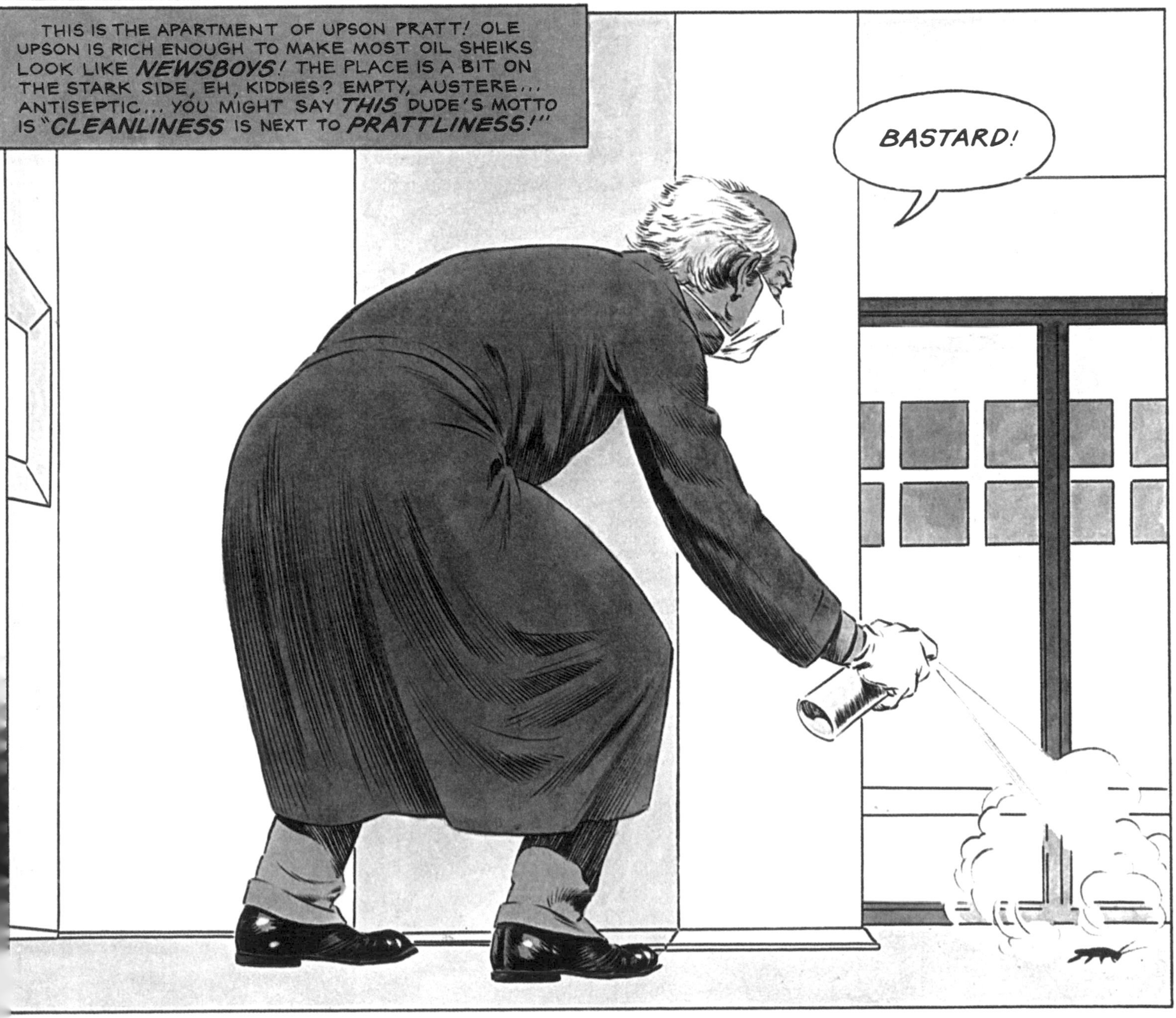
THIS IS THE APARTMENT OF UPSON PRATT! OLE UPSON IS RICH ENOUGH TO MAKE MOST OIL SHEIKS LOOK LIKE NEWSBOYS! THE PLACE IS A BIT ON THE STARK SIDE, EH, KIDDIES? EMPTY, AUSTERE... ANTISEPTIC... YOU MIGHT SAY THIS DUDE'S MOTTO IS "CLEANLINESS IS NEXT TO PRATTLINESS!"
BASTARD!

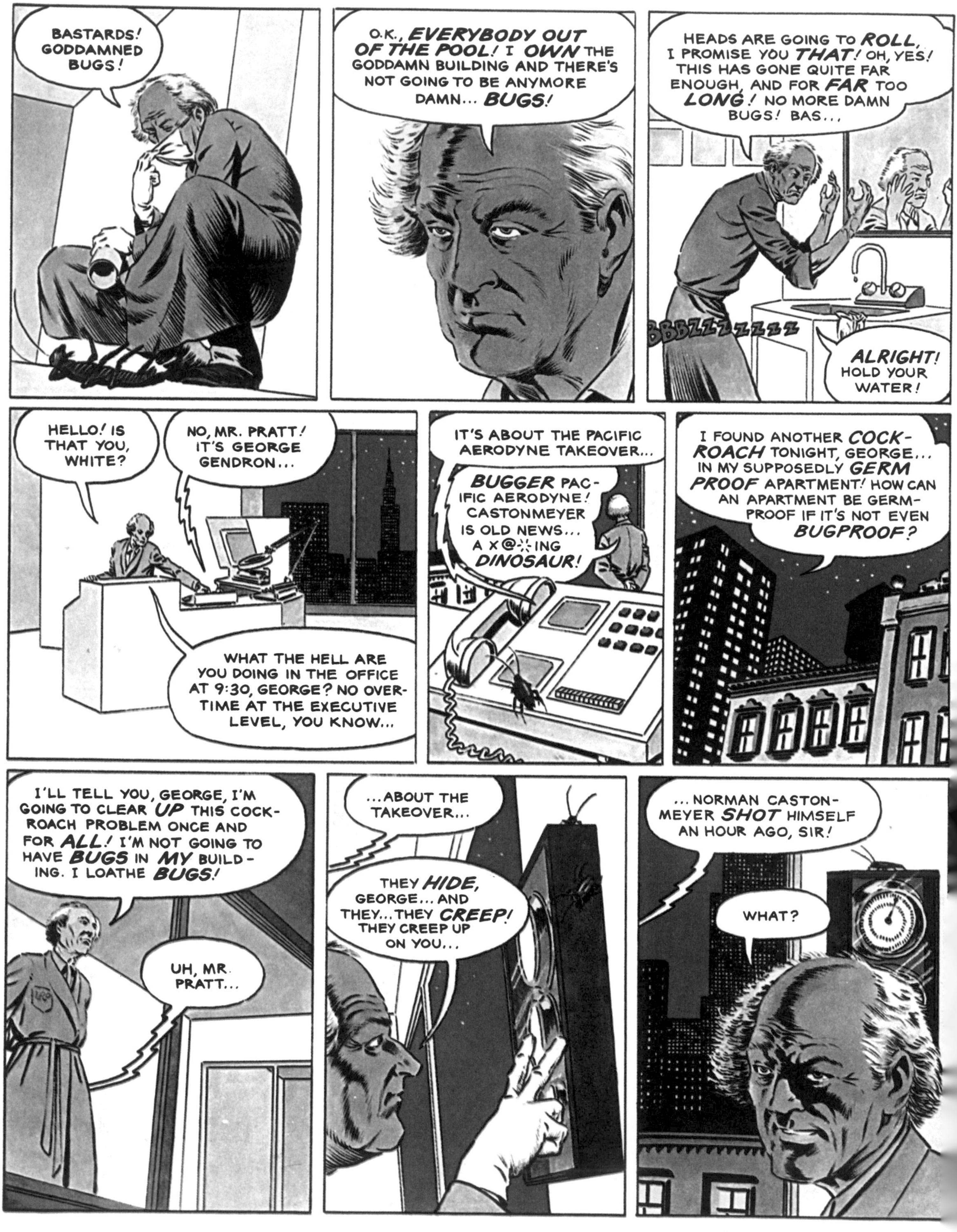
BASTARDS! GODDAMNED BUGS!
O.K., EVERYBODY OUT OF THE POOL! I OWN THE GODDAMN BUILDING AND THERE'S NOT GOING TO BE ANYMORE DAMN... BUGS!
HEADS ARE GOING TO ROLL, I PROMISE YOU THAT! OH, YES! THIS HAS GONE QUITE FAR ENOUGH, AND FOR FAR TOO LONG! NO MORE DAMN BUGS! BAS...
BBBZZZzzzzz
ALRIGHT! HOLD YOUR WATER!
HELLO! IS THAT YOU, WHITE?
NO, MR. PRATT! IT'S GEORGE GENDRON...
WHAT THE HELL ARE YOU DOING IN THE OFFICE AT 9:30, GEORGE? NO OVER-TIME AT THE EXECUTIVE LEVEL, YOU KNOW...
IT'S ABOUT THE PACIFIC AERODYNE TAKEOVER...
BUGGER PACIFIC AERODYNE! CASTONMEYER IS OLD NEWS... A X@*ING DINOSAUR!
I FOUND ANOTHER COCKROACH TONIGHT, GEORGE... IN MY SUPPOSEDLY GERM PROOF APARTMENT! HOW CAN AN APARTMENT BE GERM-PROOF IF IT'S NOT EVEN BUGPROOF?
I'LL TELL YOU, GEORGE, I'M GOING TO CLEAR UP THIS COCKROACH PROBLEM ONCE AND FOR ALL! I'M NOT GOING TO HAVE BUGS IN MY BUILDING. I LOATHE BUGS!
UH, MR. PRATT...
...ABOUT THE TAKEOVER...
THEY HIDE, GEORGE... AND THEY... THEY CREEP! THEY CREEP UP ON YOU...
...NORMAN CASTONMEYER SHOT HIMSELF AN HOUR AGO, SIR!
WHAT?

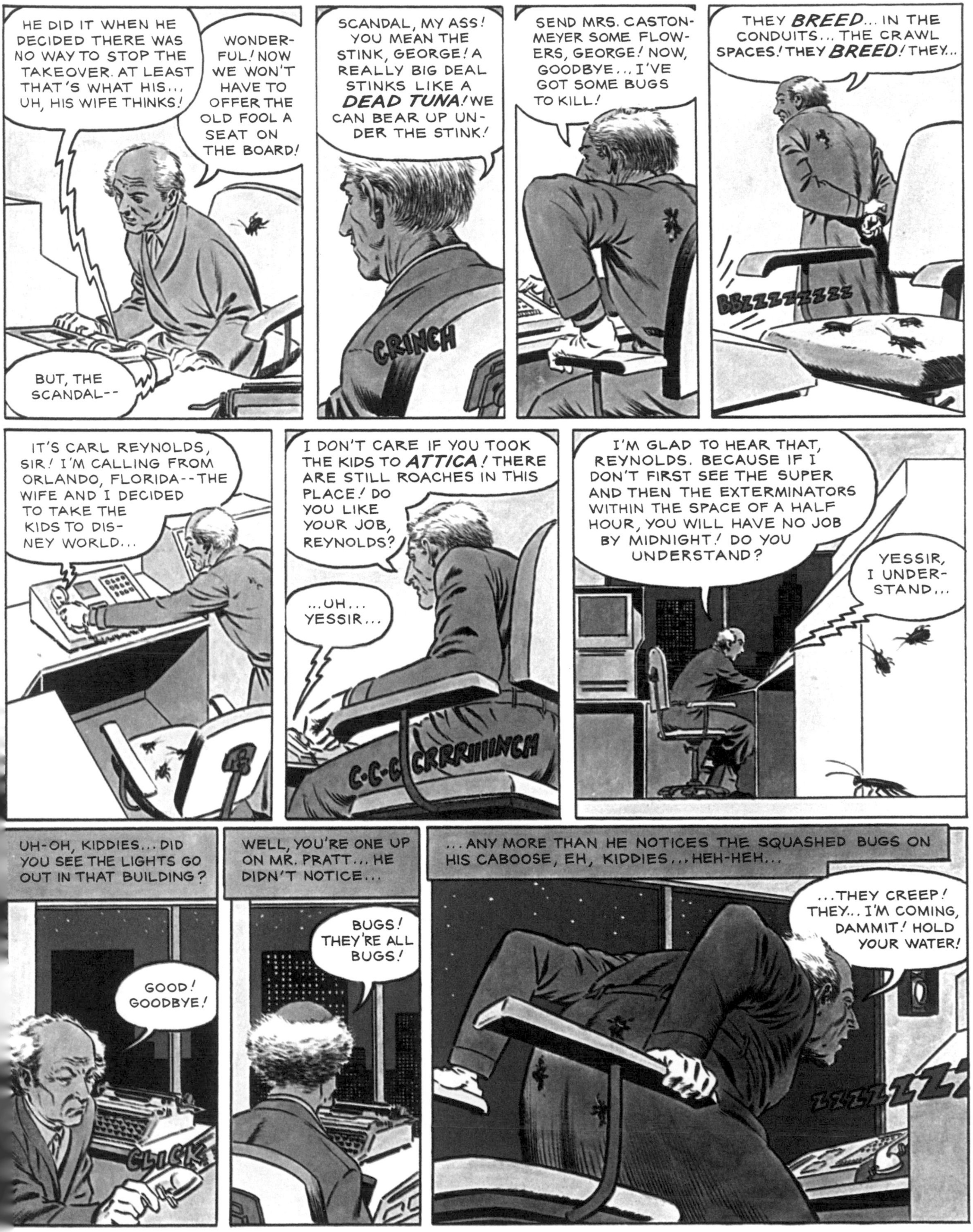
HE DID IT WHEN HE DECIDED THERE WAS NO WAY TO STOP THE TAKEOVER. AT LEAST THAT'S WHAT HIS... UH, HIS WIFE THINKS!
WONDERFUL! NOW WE WON'T HAVE TO OFFER THE OLD FOOL A SEAT ON THE BOARD!
BUT, THE SCANDAL--
SCANDAL, MY ASS! YOU MEAN THE STINK, GEORGE! A REALLY BIG DEAL STINKS LIKE A DEAD TUNA! WE CAN BEAR UP UNDER THE STINK!
CRINCH
SEND MRS. CASTONMEYER SOME FLOWERS, GEORGE! NOW, GOODBYE... I'VE GOT SOME BUGS TO KILL!
THEY BREED... IN THE CONDUITS... THE CRAWL SPACES! THEY BREED! THEY...
BBZZZZZZZZZ
IT'S CARL REYNOLDS, SIR! I'M CALLING FROM ORLANDO, FLORIDA--THE WIFE AND I DECIDED TO TAKE THE KIDS TO DISNEY WORLD...
I DON'T CARE IF YOU TOOK THE KIDS TO ATTICA! THERE ARE STILL ROACHES IN THIS PLACE! DO YOU LIKE YOUR JOB, REYNOLDS?
...UH... YESSIR...
C-C-C CRRRIIIINCH
I'M GLAD TO HEAR THAT, REYNOLDS. BECAUSE IF I DON'T FIRST SEE THE SUPER AND THEN THE EXTERMINATORS WITHIN THE SPACE OF A HALF HOUR, YOU WILL HAVE NO JOB BY MIDNIGHT! DO YOU UNDERSTAND?
YESSIR, I UNDERSTAND...
UH-OH, KIDDIES... DID YOU SEE THE LIGHTS GO OUT IN THAT BUILDING?
GOOD! GOODBYE!
CLICK
WELL, YOU'RE ONE UP ON MR. PRATT... HE DIDN'T NOTICE...
BUGS! THEY'RE ALL BUGS!
...ANY MORE THAN HE NOTICES THE SQUASHED BUGS ON HIS CABOOSE, EH, KIDDIES... HEH-HEH...
...THEY CREEP! THEY... I'M COMING, DAMMIT! HOLD YOUR WATER!
ZZZZZZZ

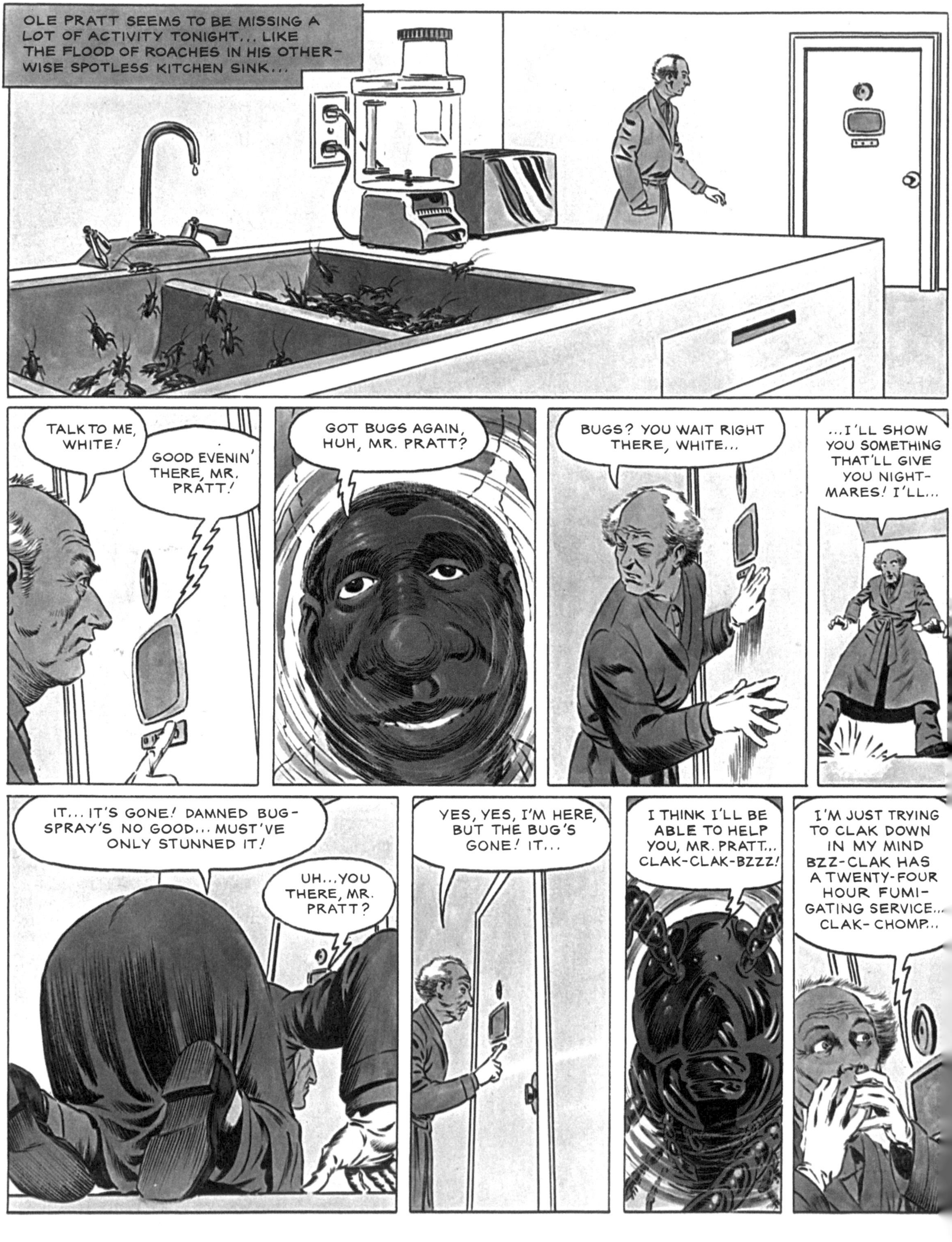
OLE PRATT SEEMS TO BE MISSING A LOT OF ACTIVITY TONIGHT... LIKE THE FLOOD OF ROACHES IN HIS OTHERWISE SPOTLESS KITCHEN SINK...
TALK TO ME, WHITE!
GOOD EVENIN' THERE, MR. PRATT!
GOT BUGS AGAIN, HUH, MR. PRATT?
BUGS? YOU WAIT RIGHT THERE, WHITE...
...I'LL SHOW YOU SOMETHING THAT'LL GIVE YOU NIGHTMARES! I'LL...
IT... IT'S GONE! DAMNED BUG-SPRAY'S NO GOOD... MUST'VE ONLY STUNNED IT!
UH...YOU THERE, MR. PRATT?
YES, YES, I'M HERE, BUT THE BUG'S GONE! IT...
I THINK I'LL BE ABLE TO HELP YOU, MR. PRATT... CLAK-CLAK-BZZZ!
I'M JUST TRYING TO CLAK DOWN IN MY MIND BZZ-CLAK HAS A TWENTY-FOUR HOUR FUMIGATING SERVICE... CLAK-CHOMP...

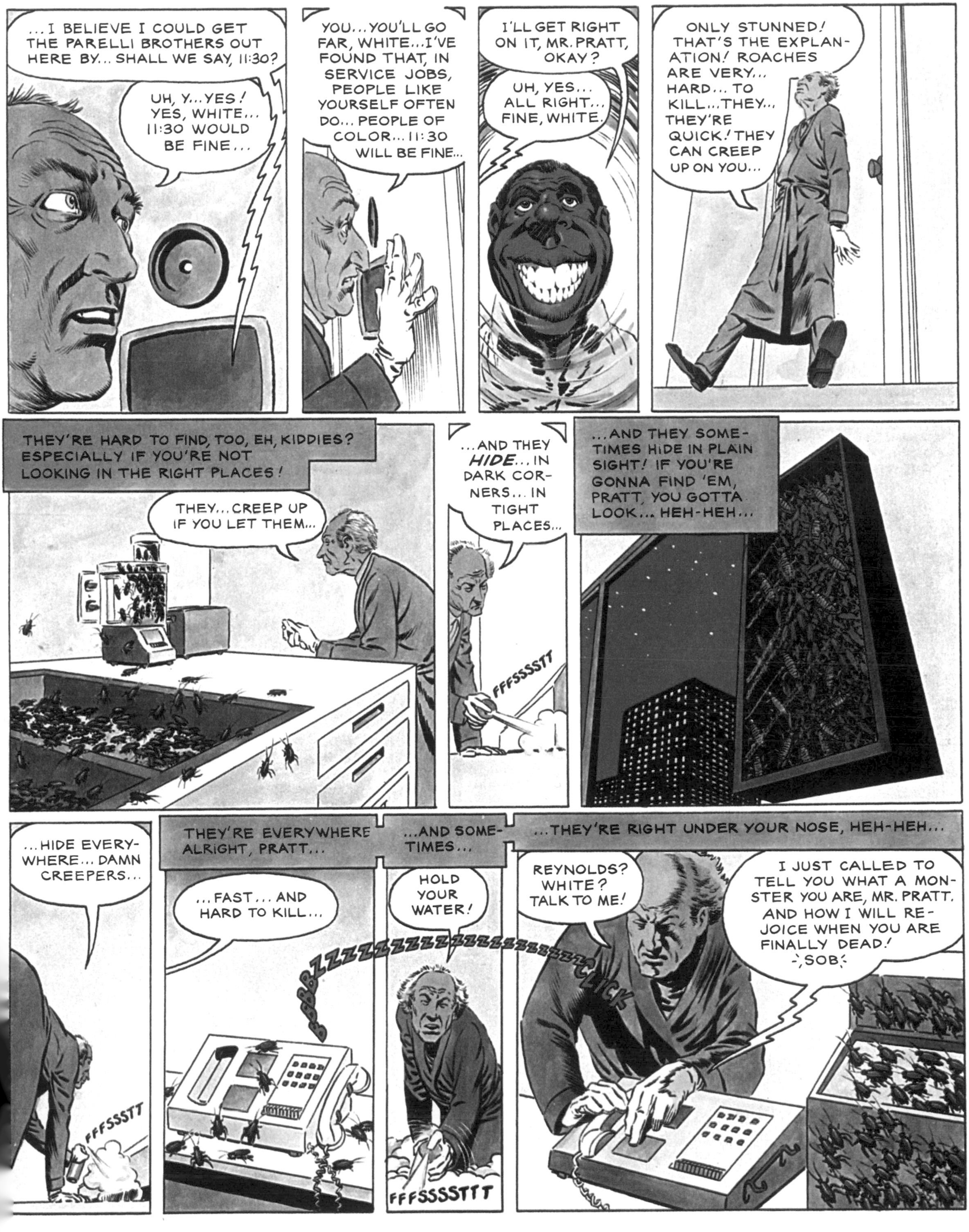
...I BELIEVE I COULD GET THE PARELLI BROTHERS OUT HERE BY... SHALL WE SAY, 11:30?
UH, Y...YES! YES, WHITE... 11:30 WOULD BE FINE...
YOU...YOU'LL GO FAR, WHITE...I'VE FOUND THAT, IN SERVICE JOBS, PEOPLE LIKE YOURSELF OFTEN DO... PEOPLE OF COLOR... 11:30 WILL BE FINE...
I'LL GET RIGHT ON IT, MR. PRATT, OKAY?
UH, YES... ALL RIGHT... FINE, WHITE.
ONLY STUNNED! THAT'S THE EXPLANATION! ROACHES ARE VERY... HARD... TO KILL... THEY... THEY'RE QUICK! THEY CAN CREEP UP ON YOU...
THEY'RE HARD TO FIND, TOO, EH, KIDDIES? ESPECIALLY IF YOU'RE NOT LOOKING IN THE RIGHT PLACES!
THEY... CREEP UP IF YOU LET THEM...
...AND THEY HIDE... IN DARK CORNERS... IN TIGHT PLACES...
FFFSSSSTT
...AND THEY SOMETIMES HIDE IN PLAIN SIGHT! IF YOU'RE GONNA FIND 'EM, PRATT, YOU GOTTA LOOK... HEH-HEH...
...HIDE EVERYWHERE... DAMN CREEPERS...
FFFSSSTT
THEY'RE EVERYWHERE ALRIGHT, PRATT...
...AND SOMETIMES...
...THEY'RE RIGHT UNDER YOUR NOSE, HEH-HEH...
...FAST... AND HARD TO KILL...
BBBBZZZZZZZZZZZZZZZZZZZZ
HOLD YOUR WATER!
FFFSSSSTTT
REYNOLDS? WHITE? TALK TO ME!
CLICK
I JUST CALLED TO TELL YOU WHAT A MONSTER YOU ARE, MR. PRATT. AND HOW I WILL REJOICE WHEN YOU ARE FINALLY DEAD! -SOB-

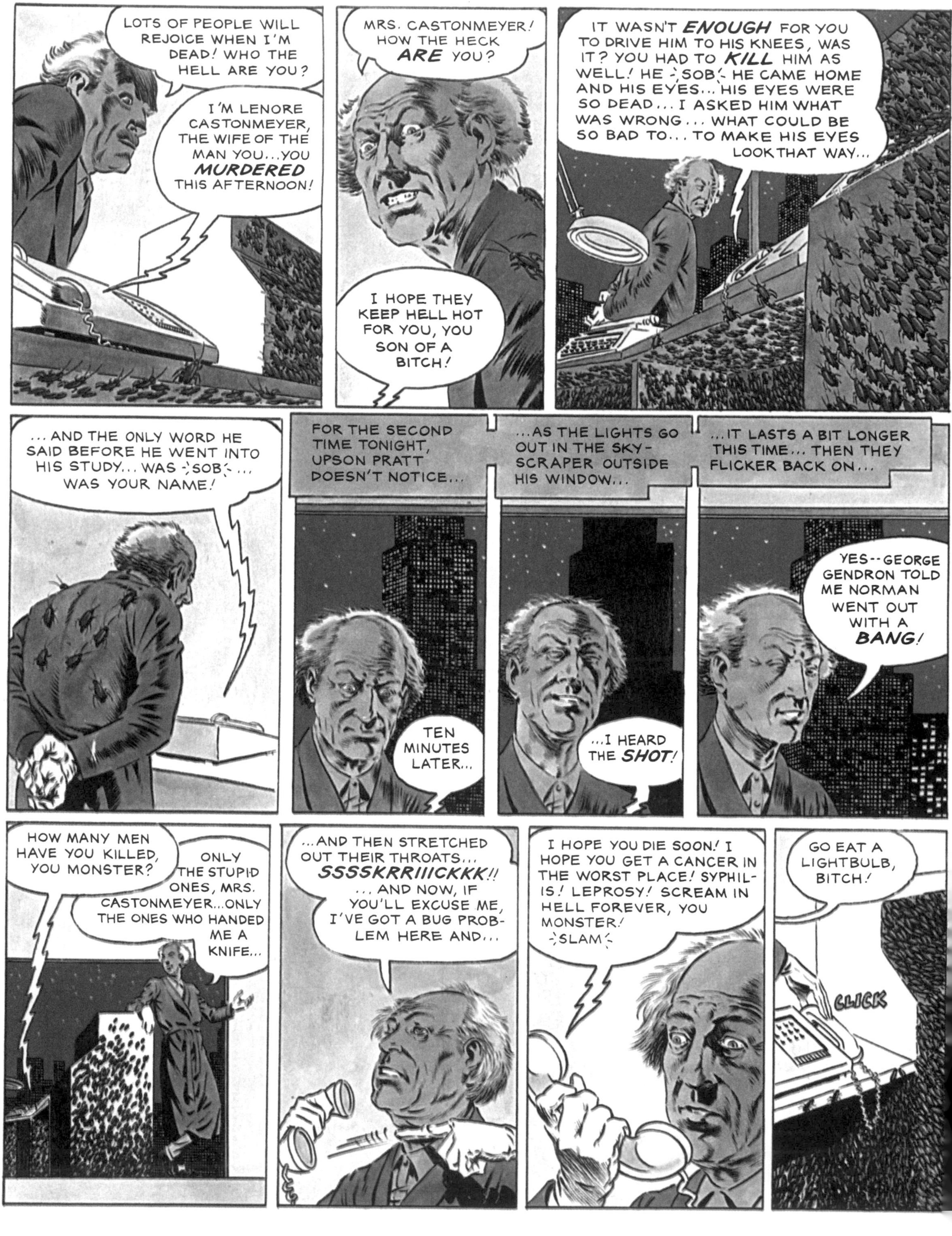

LOTS OF PEOPLE WILL REJOICE WHEN I'M DEAD! WHO THE HELL ARE YOU?
I'M LENORE CASTONMEYER, THE WIFE OF THE MAN YOU...YOU MURDERED THIS AFTERNOON!
MRS. CASTONMEYER! HOW THE HECK ARE YOU?
I HOPE THEY KEEP HELL HOT FOR YOU, YOU SON OF A BITCH!
IT WASN'T ENOUGH FOR YOU TO DRIVE HIM TO HIS KNEES, WAS IT? YOU HAD TO KILL HIM AS WELL! HE -SOB- HE CAME HOME AND HIS EYES... HIS EYES WERE SO DEAD... I ASKED HIM WHAT WAS WRONG... WHAT COULD BE SO BAD TO... TO MAKE HIS EYES LOOK THAT WAY...
...AND THE ONLY WORD HE SAID BEFORE HE WENT INTO HIS STUDY... WAS -SOB- ... WAS YOUR NAME!
FOR THE SECOND TIME TONIGHT, UPSON PRATT DOESN'T NOTICE...
TEN MINUTES LATER...
...AS THE LIGHTS GO OUT IN THE SKY-SCRAPER OUTSIDE HIS WINDOW...
...I HEARD THE SHOT!
...IT LASTS A BIT LONGER THIS TIME... THEN THEY FLICKER BACK ON...
YES--GEORGE GENDRON TOLD ME NORMAN WENT OUT WITH A BANG!
HOW MANY MEN HAVE YOU KILLED, YOU MONSTER?
ONLY THE STUPID ONES, MRS. CASTONMEYER...ONLY THE ONES WHO HANDED ME A KNIFE...
...AND THEN STRETCHED OUT THEIR THROATS... SSSSKRRIIICKKK!! ...AND NOW, IF YOU'LL EXCUSE ME, I'VE GOT A BUG PROB-LEM HERE AND...
I HOPE YOU DIE SOON! I HOPE YOU GET A CANCER IN THE WORST PLACE! SYPHIL-IS! LEPROSY! SCREAM IN HELL FOREVER, YOU MONSTER!
-SLAM-
GO EAT A LIGHTBULB, BITCH!
CLICK

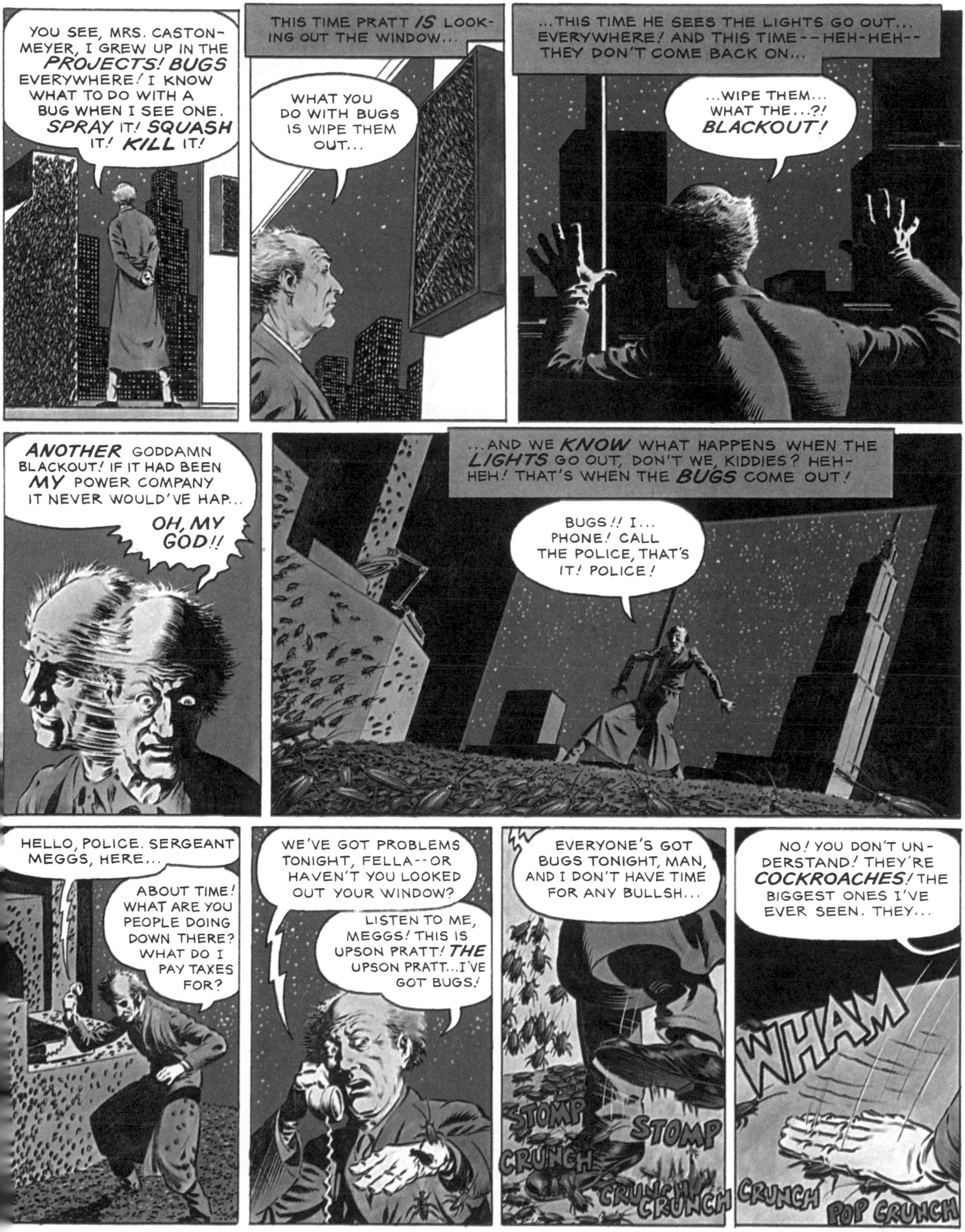
YOU SEE, MRS. CASTON-MEYER, I GREW UP IN THE PROJECTS! BUGS EVERYWHERE! I KNOW WHAT TO DO WITH A BUG WHEN I SEE ONE. SPRAY IT! SQUASH IT! KILL IT!
THIS TIME PRATT IS LOOKING OUT THE WINDOW...
WHAT YOU DO WITH BUGS IS WIPE THEM OUT...
...THIS TIME HE SEES THE LIGHTS GO OUT... EVERYWHERE! AND THIS TIME--HEH-HEH--THEY DON'T COME BACK ON...
...WIPE THEM... WHAT THE...?! BLACKOUT!
ANOTHER GODDAMN BLACKOUT! IF IT HAD BEEN MY POWER COMPANY IT NEVER WOULD'VE HAP...
OH, MY GOD!!
...AND WE KNOW WHAT HAPPENS WHEN THE LIGHTS GO OUT, DON'T WE, KIDDIES? HEH-HEH! THAT'S WHEN THE BUGS COME OUT!
BUGS!! I... PHONE! CALL THE POLICE, THAT'S IT! POLICE!
HELLO, POLICE. SERGEANT MEGGS, HERE...
ABOUT TIME! WHAT ARE YOU PEOPLE DOING DOWN THERE? WHAT DO I PAY TAXES FOR?
WE'VE GOT PROBLEMS TONIGHT, FELLA--OR HAVEN'T YOU LOOKED OUT YOUR WINDOW?
LISTEN TO ME, MEGGS! THIS IS UPSON PRATT! THE UPSON PRATT...I'VE GOT BUGS!
EVERYONE'S GOT BUGS TONIGHT, MAN, AND I DON'T HAVE TIME FOR ANY BULLSH...
STOMP
STOMP
CRUNCH
CRUNCH CRUNCH
NO! YOU DON'T UNDERSTAND! THEY'RE COCKROACHES! THE BIGGEST ONES I'VE EVER SEEN. THEY...
WHAM
CRUNCH
POP CRUNCH

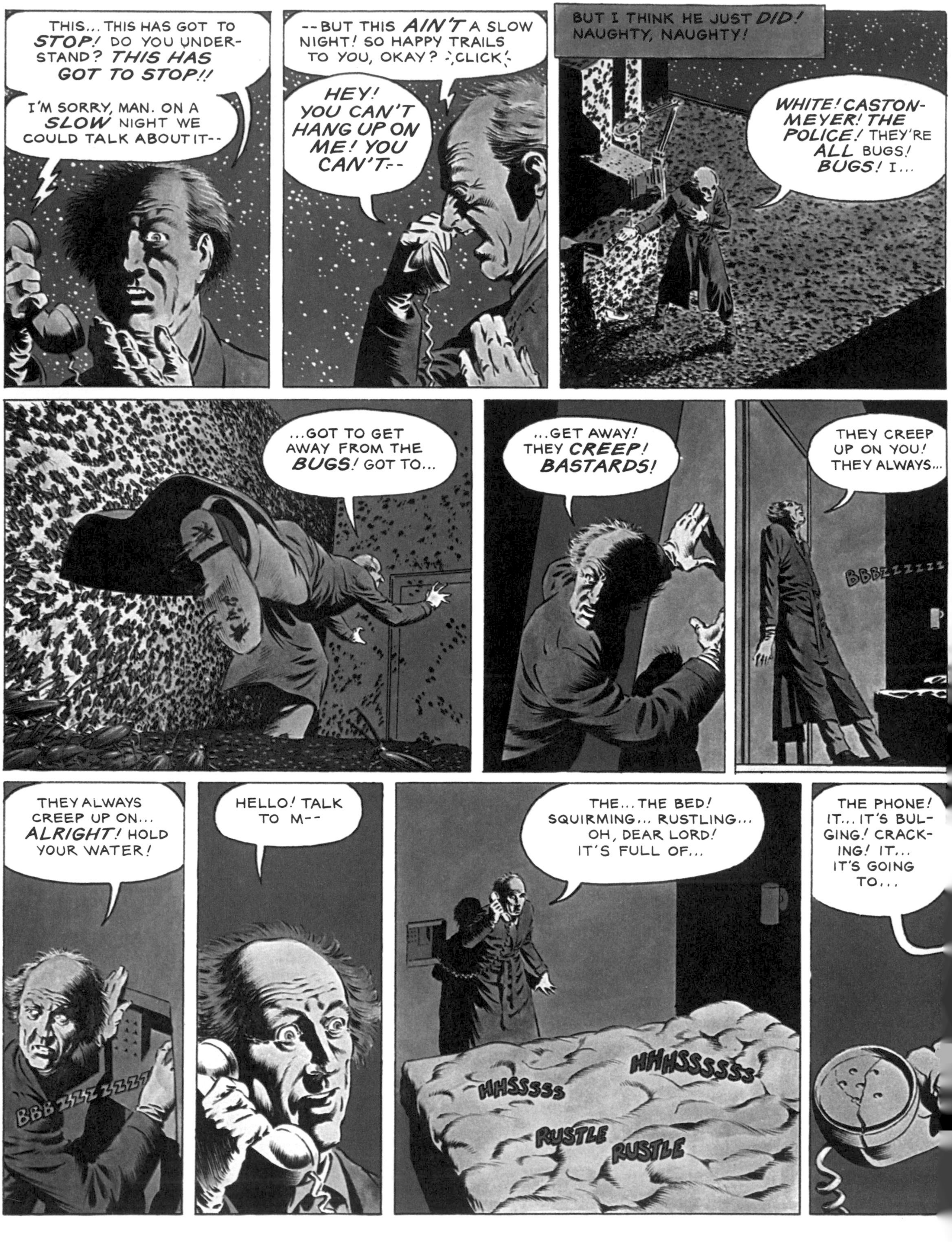
THIS... THIS HAS GOT TO STOP! DO YOU UNDERSTAND? THIS HAS GOT TO STOP!!
I'M SORRY, MAN. ON A SLOW NIGHT WE COULD TALK ABOUT IT--
--BUT THIS AIN'T A SLOW NIGHT! SO HAPPY TRAILS TO YOU, OKAY? CLICK
HEY! YOU CAN'T HANG UP ON ME! YOU CAN'T--
BUT I THINK HE JUST DID! NAUGHTY, NAUGHTY!
WHITE! CASTONMEYER! THE POLICE! THEY'RE ALL BUGS! BUGS! I...
...GOT TO GET AWAY FROM THE BUGS! GOT TO...
...GET AWAY! THEY CREEP! BASTARDS!
THEY CREEP UP ON YOU! THEY ALWAYS...
BBBZZZZZZ
THEY ALWAYS CREEP UP ON... ALRIGHT! HOLD YOUR WATER!
BBBZZZZZZZZ
HELLO! TALK TO M--
THE... THE BED! SQUIRMING... RUSTLING... OH, DEAR LORD! IT'S FULL OF...
HHSSSSS
HHHSSSSSSS
RUSTLE
RUSTLE
THE PHONE! IT... IT'S BULGING! CRACKING! IT... IT'S GOING TO...

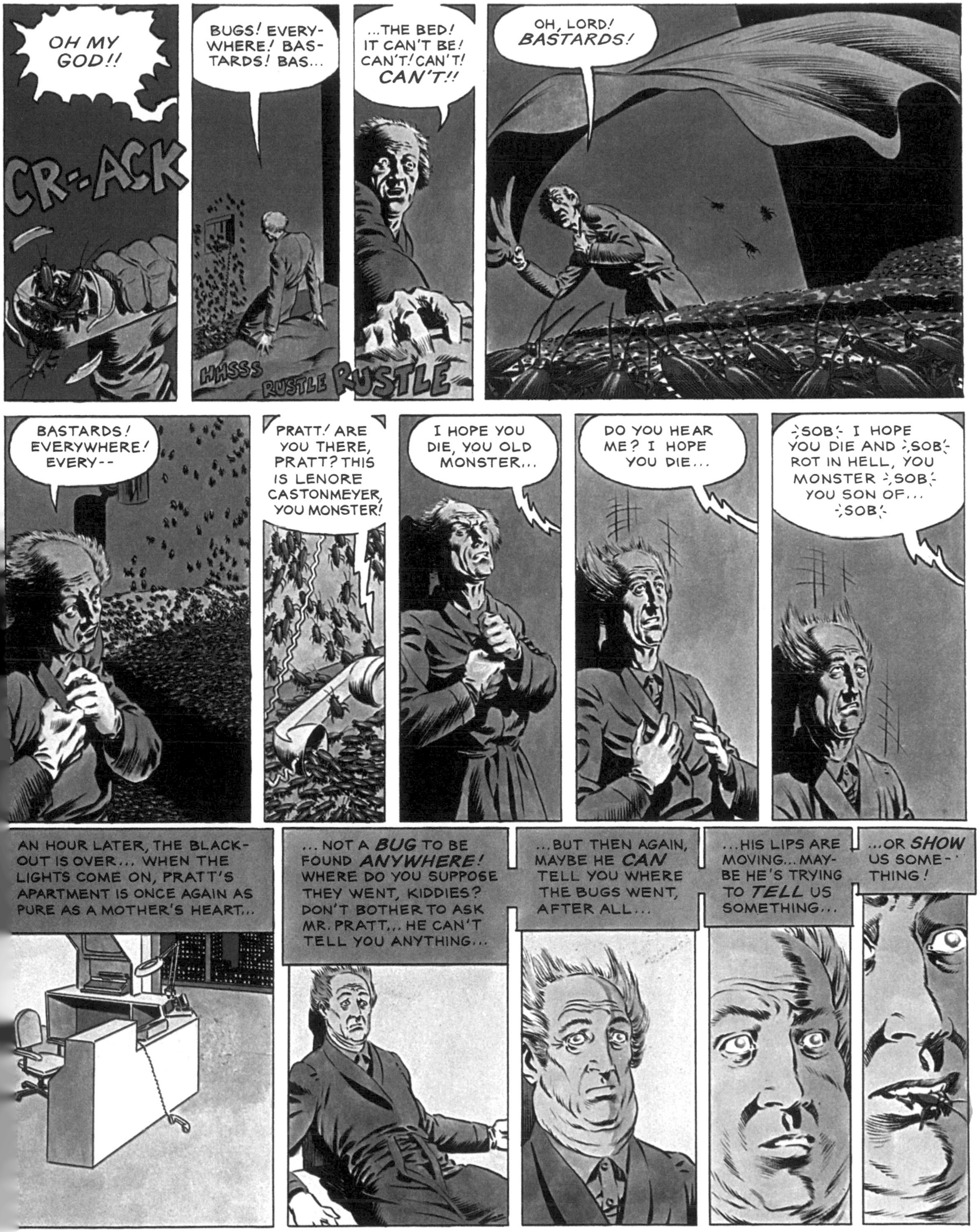

OH MY GOD!!
CR-ACK
BUGS! EVERYWHERE! BASTARDS! BAS...
HHSSS
RUSTLE RUSTLE
...THE BED! IT CAN'T BE! CAN'T! CAN'T! CAN'T!!
OH, LORD! BASTARDS!
BASTARDS! EVERYWHERE! EVERY--
PRATT! ARE YOU THERE, PRATT? THIS IS LENORE CASTONMEYER, YOU MONSTER!
I HOPE YOU DIE, YOU OLD MONSTER...
DO YOU HEAR ME? I HOPE YOU DIE...
SOB I HOPE YOU DIE AND SOB ROT IN HELL, YOU MONSTER SOB YOU SON OF... SOB
AN HOUR LATER, THE BLACKOUT IS OVER... WHEN THE LIGHTS COME ON, PRATT'S APARTMENT IS ONCE AGAIN AS PURE AS A MOTHER'S HEART...
... NOT A BUG TO BE FOUND ANYWHERE! WHERE DO YOU SUPPOSE THEY WENT, KIDDIES? DON'T BOTHER TO ASK MR. PRATT... HE CAN'T TELL YOU ANYTHING...
...BUT THEN AGAIN, MAYBE HE CAN TELL YOU WHERE THE BUGS WENT, AFTER ALL...
...HIS LIPS ARE MOVING... MAYBE HE'S TRYING TO TELL US SOMETHING...
...OR SHOW US SOMETHING!

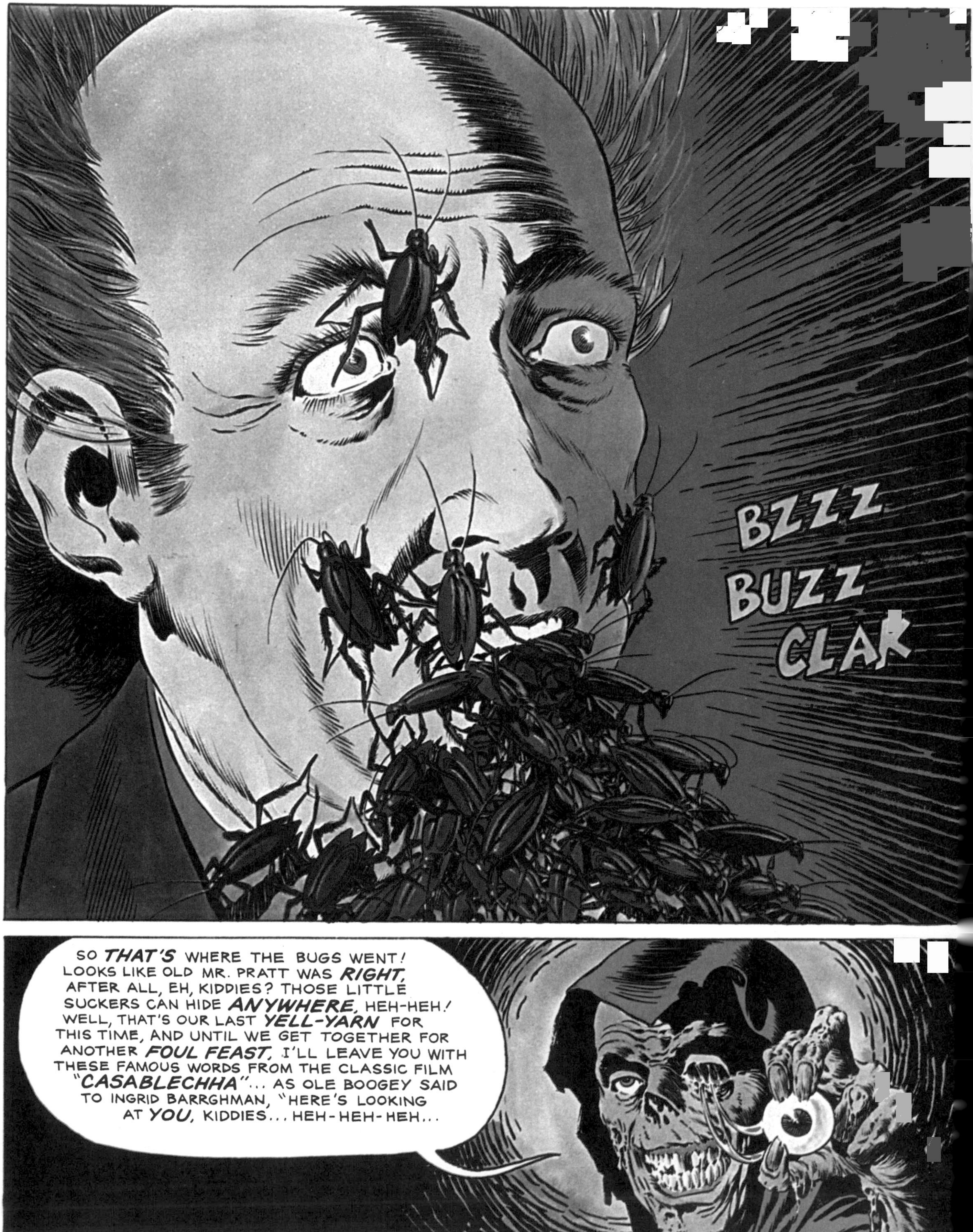
BZZZ
BUZZ
CLAK
SO THAT'S WHERE THE BUGS WENT! LOOKS LIKE OLD MR. PRATT WAS RIGHT, AFTER ALL, EH, KIDDIES? THOSE LITTLE SUCKERS CAN HIDE ANYWHERE, HEH-HEH! WELL, THAT'S OUR LAST YELL-YARN FOR THIS TIME, AND UNTIL WE GET TOGETHER FOR ANOTHER FOUL FEAST, I'LL LEAVE YOU WITH THESE FAMOUS WORDS FROM THE CLASSIC FILM "CASABLECHHA"... AS OLE BOOGEY SAID TO INGRID BARRGHMAN, "HERE'S LOOKING AT YOU, KIDDIES... HEH-HEH-HEH...

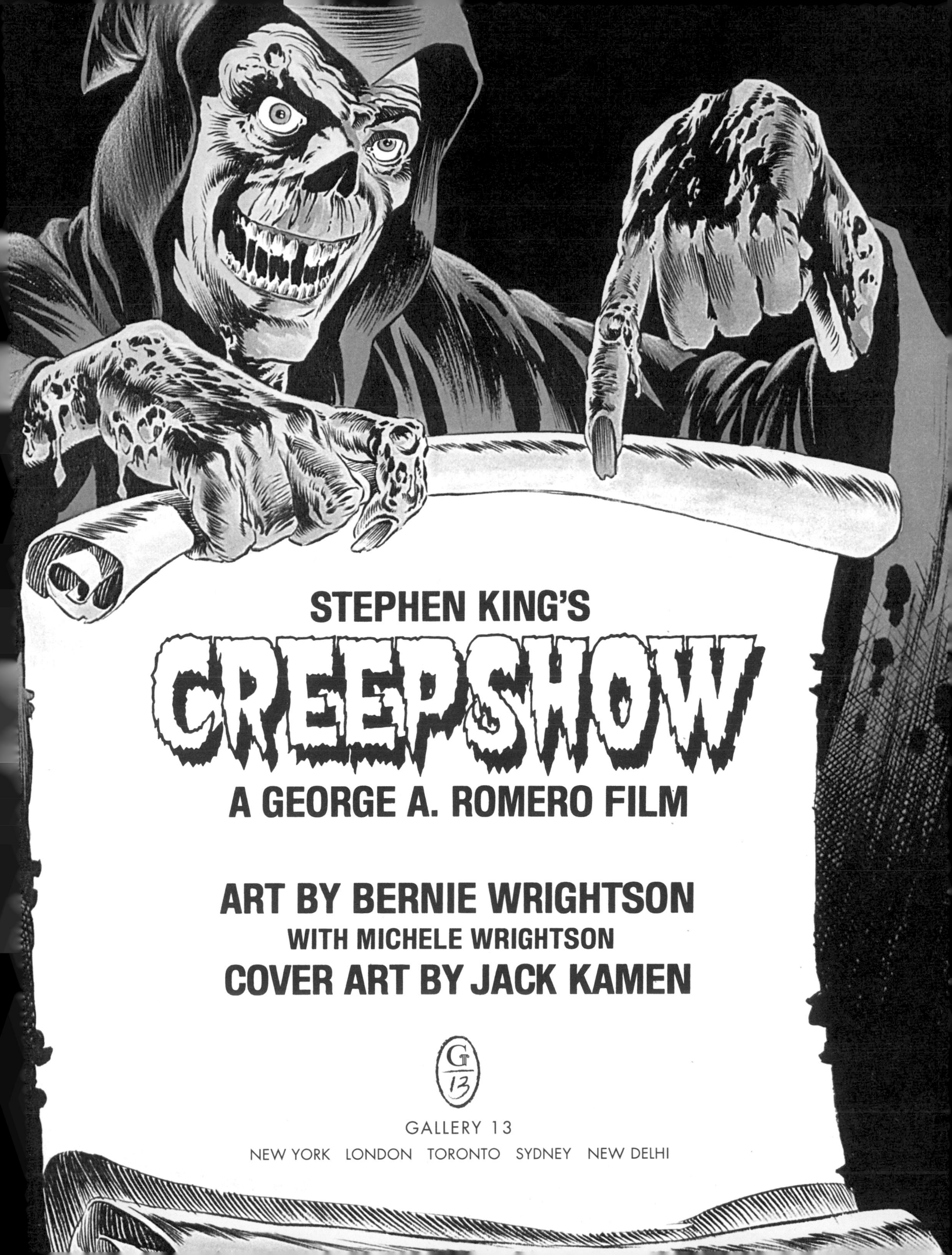

STEPHEN KING'S

CREEPSHOW

A GEORGE A. ROMERO FILM

ART BY BERNIE WRIGHTSON
WITH MICHELE WRIGHTSON
COVER ART BY JACK KAMEN

GALLERY 13
NEW YORK LONDON TORONTO SYDNEY NEW DELHI

Gallery 13
An Imprint of Simon & Schuster, Inc.
1230 Avenue of the Americas
New York, NY 10020

Copyright © 1982 by Philtrum Corp.
Illustrations copyright © 1982 by Laurel-Show, Inc.

First Gallery 13 trade paperback edition May 2017

GALLERY 13 and colophon are registered trademarks of Simon & Schuster, Inc.

For information about special discounts for bulk purchases,
please contact Simon & Schuster Special Sales at 1-866-506-1949
or business@simonandschuster.com.

The Simon & Schuster Speakers Bureau can bring authors to
your live event. For more information or to book an event, contact
the Simon & Schuster Speakers Bureau at 1-866-248-3049 or
visit our website at www.simonspeakers.com.

Manufactured in the United States of America

10 9 8 7 6 5 4 3

ISBN 978-1-5011-6322-7
ISBN 978-1-5011-4129-4 (ebook)